The Naomi Poems: Book One: Corpse and Beans

Auto-necrophilia

Nights of Naomi

Love Poems to Myself

Rome in Rome

Selected and Collected Poems

Becos

Outremer

Poems 1963–1988

The Quicken Tree

Laugh at the End of the World: Collected Comic Poems 1969–1999

The Unsubscriber

I AM FLYING INTO MYSELF

I AM FLYING INTO MYSELF

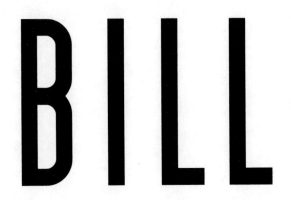

BILL

FARRAR STRAUS GIROUX / NEW YORK

SELECTED POEMS, 1960–2014

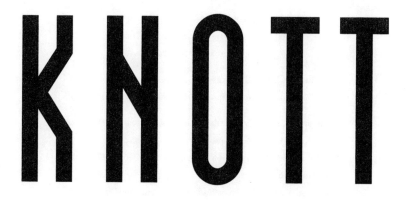

EDITED AND WITH AN
INTRODUCTION BY THOMAS LUX

Farrar, Straus and Giroux

175 Varick Street, New York 10014

Printed in the United States of America

Published in 2017 by Farrar, Straus and Giroux

First paperback edition, 2018

Grateful acknowledgment is made to Big Table Books for permission to
reprint poems from *The Naomi Poems* (1968) and *Auto-necrophilia* (1971).

The Library of Congress has cataloged the hardcover edition as follows:

Names: Knott, Bill, 1940–2014 author. | Lux, Thomas, 1946–

Title: I am flying into myself : selected poems, 1960–2014 / Bill Knott;
    edited by Thomas Lux.

Description: First edition. | New York : Farrar, Straus and Giroux, 2017.

Identifiers: LCCN 2016031333 | ISBN 9780374260675 (hardback) |
    ISBN 9780374714758 (e-book)

Subjects: BISAC: POETRY / American / General.

Classification: LCC PS3561.N65 A6 2017 | DDC 811/.54—dc23

LC record available at https://lccn.loc.gov/2016031333

Paperback ISBN: 978-0-374-53752-4

Designed by Quemadura

Our books may be purchased in bulk for promotional, educational, or
business use. Please contact your local bookseller or the Macmillan Corporate
and Premium Sales Department at 1-800-221-7945, extension 5442,
or by e-mail at MacmillanSpecialMarkets@macmillan.com.

www.fsgbooks.com

www.twitter.com/fsgbooks

www.facebook.com/fsgbooks

1 3 5 7 9 10 8 6 4 2

CONTENTS

INTRODUCTION

I met Bill Knott in late 1968, or in early 1969, at William Corbett's house, a gathering place for poets in Boston's South End. I'd read Knott's highly acclaimed first book, *The Naomi Poems*, from Big Table, in the spring of 1968. It was published under the pen name St. Geraud (1940–1966). I was immediately struck, poleaxed, by the emotional power of the poems. Mostly short, intense lyrics, they were unlike anything I'd ever read and moved me to the bone. I felt, before I'd read Emily Dickinson's famous comment, as if the top of my head was taken off. Many were love poems. Most were written in his early and mid-twenties. There was urgency, a longing, a wild and plaintive high-note sound that was maybe particularly attractive to a twenty-two-year-old man. Forty-seven years later, as I stand on the terrible threshold of senescence, Knott's poems still lift the hairs on the back of my neck. His anguished poems about the war in Vietnam were among the first I'd read on that subject, and I still believe them to be among the strongest. It is the war that my generation either can't forget or refuses to remember (sometimes both).

Unfortunately, he also wrote in one poem that he couldn't see the difference between several prominent American poets and "aviators dropping a bomb on Vietnamese women and children."* This was egregiously rude, of course, and flat-out dumb, not to mention self-destructive, and added more to the controversy of early Bill Knott.

*"I Don't Know," from *The Naomi Poems* (Chicago: Big Table Publishing Co., 1968), pp. 54–55.

By December 1970, Knott was living on a couch in the kitchen of the apartment my college roommate and I rented in Somerville, Massachusetts. Sometime in early 1971, he published his second book, *Auto-necrophilia*, also with Big Table. This was a thinner book than *The Naomi Poems*. He was flat broke and needed the $800 advance— enough to eat and pay rent for several months.

My college roommate and friend, Joseph Wilmott, and I started a small press (Barn Dream Press) around this time. Between 1970 and 1974, we published two of Knott's books. The first was *Nights of Naomi*, published in early 1971. By this time, Knott had dropped "St. Geraud" but, still claiming posthumousness, was now Bill Knott (1940–1966). The second book, *Love Poems to Myself*, was published in 1974 under the name he used for the rest of his life: Bill Knott.

William Kilborn Knott was born in Carson City, Michigan, on February 17, 1940. He died in Bay City, Michigan, after failed heart surgery, on March 12, 2014. When he was seven, his mother died while giving birth; the child also died. His father, a butcher, died by drinking poison three years later. Knott told me that he believed his father's manner of death caused the chronic stomach problems he himself suffered throughout his life. When his father died, Knott was already in an orphanage (for reasons "too complex to explain"*) run by the Loyal Order of Moose, in Mooseheart, Illinois. There, for several years, he was bullied and abused. He was sent for a year to a state mental hospital, where he was also bullied and abused. His uncle got him out, and he lived on the uncle's farm for a few years before he joined the U.S. Army in the late 1950s. He served his full enlistment and was honorably discharged in 1960. A great deal of his service time was spent

*From "The Day After My Father's Death"; see page 25.

guarding our nation's gold reserves at Fort Knox. He liked to say the greens and fairways of the officers' golf course were always dry and snow-free in winter, the heat from the bullion in the vaults beneath keeping them so.

The last time he saw his younger sister, Joy, was when she "graduated" from the orphanage at nineteen. He had a niece and nephew he never met.

By the early 1960s, Knott was living in Chicago and working as a hospital orderly. He took a poetry workshop taught by John Logan, and a little later worked with Paul Carroll, editor of Big Table Books. Some of the poets in Chicago who knew Knott at the time were Charles Simic, Kathleen Norris, Dennis Schmitz, Naomi Lazard, and William Hunt.

In 1964, James Wright received a letter from Kenneth Rexroth asking if Wright could recommend some younger poets to him. Wright wrote back about "an unmistakably beautiful, deeply fertile, unaffected, marvelous poet, . . . a young man of about 25 years of age who has the wonderfully unpoetick name of *Bill Knott*."*

Enough has been said about a letter Knott wrote to a magazine, in 1962 or 1963, under a fictitious name, saying that Bill Knott was dead and died "a virgin and a suicide." It was despair and a youthful affectation. And let literary history acknowledge this obvious fact: Being a young poet, particularly a young male poet, is almost a *disease*, a cement mixer of joy rip-sawed by a realistic sense of the impossibility of the task! Knott said he used St. Geraud as a pen name because even though he was honorably discharged from the army, he never reported

*A Wild Perfection: The Selected Letters of James Wright, ed. Anne Wright and Saundra Rose Mailey (New York: Farrar, Straus and Giroux, 2005), p. 293.

for reserve duty and thought the army might track him down and make him return to active duty. When he told me this, I remember thinking: Of course, the army has a special unit scouring first books of poetry looking for reprobates like Bill.

When asked, years later, why he used a pen name, he said it was because two poets he admired—Pablo Neruda and Paul Éluard—were pen-named poets, and that made him feel justified. We should look at the pen name in a similar manner as the fake suicide letter: So what!

St. Geraud, by the way, was the name of a character he lifted from a nineteenth-century pornographic novel, the kind in which it takes forty pages to get the top button of a woman's blouse unbuttoned.

I thought one of Knott's reasons for insisting that his name include "(1940–1966)" made some odd sense: He believed all Americans, not just combatants, were casualties of the Vietnam War, because, as Americans, we all shared the responsibility for and were all wounded by that illegal and immoral war. Hyperbole, of course. He knew where the real blame lay: "there are the destroyers—the Johnsons, Kys, Rusks, Hitlers, Francos—then there are / those they want to destroy—lovers, teachers, plows, potatoes."* Therefore, Knott said, all Americans should declare themselves dead and live and write from then on posthumously. Hyperbole, ditto. It's a metaphor of the absurd, but it's a readable metaphor. It's satire, bitter satire you can taste on your tongue. It's funny and dead serious: "Like a spigot on a corpse."† Or, a little more gently, "Like a water-lily on crutches."‡

---

*From "To American Poets," in *The Naomi Poems*, pp. 31–32.

†From "Whimsical Tears, Or? The Theory of Posthumous Poetry," in *Auto-necrophilia* (Chicago: Big Table, 1971), pp. 16–18.

‡From an uncollected poem.

Wilmott and I started Barn Dream Press with little money during our last semester of college. Wilmott went into the printing trade, and we published, during a four-year run, several broadsides, chapbooks, and three full-length books, by poets such as William Matthews, Charles Wright, Marvin Bell, Paul Hannigan, William Corbett, Helen Chasin, and Michael Palmer. We started working on Knott's book *Nights of Naomi* in the fall of 1970.

I was hired as a night watchman at a local college, which provided two meals a day and pilferable lightbulbs and toilet paper: I had the keys to everything. It was around this time that Knott lived on a couch in our kitchen for a few months. I'd get home about 1:00 a.m. Knott would invariably be watching old movies on two black-and-white TVs, a smaller one on top of a larger one. He got up constantly to change the channel on one or the other, while keeping the sound on only one TV.

By late January of 1971, Knott had moved to an apartment deeper into blue-collar Somerville.

Nights of Naomi was printed by letterpress on fine watermarked paper in an edition of 1,000 copies: 874 bound in blue paper, 100 hardbacks bound in dark blue boards numbered and signed, and 26 hardbacks lettered A–Z signed with a personal inscription by the author. Typical: "Larry, thanks for bailing me out of jail that night in Albany." Neither had Larry bought the book nor had Knott spent a night in jail in Albany. We later published a second edition of 1,000 copies with a completely different design and this time offset printing.

When Wilmott and I got the first hardcover copies from the bindery, we took some to Knott's apartment. It was still cold, probably March 1971. After much banging on the door, he finally let us in. All the windows were boarded up from the inside. His phone and electricity were cut off. The only room he used was the kitchen. All four burners of the gas stove were on for heat. There was a mattress on the floor. He sat on it. I forget where, or if, we sat. We handed him a copy. He flipped through the pages for a few seconds and then tossed the book over his shoulder into a pile of trash surrounding an overflowing wastebasket! He made an excuse about needing to work, and we were back on the street.

A few days or weeks later, Knott explained to me that he'd been expecting "a crummy mimeographed book." He said he was over-whelmed by how good it looked. He said he couldn't believe we cared enough about his poems to make such a well-produced book. (He might have also, legitimately, felt we weren't *capable* of produc-ing such a book.) Bill had serious self-esteem problems—and who wouldn't, given the hand he had been dealt. It became clear to me years later that Knott was then profoundly clinically depressed. It's my feeling that he lived with various levels of depression (I don't know if he was ever treated for it) for the rest of his life.

It should be noted that, in an age of massive self-medication, Knott very rarely drank alcohol, and he stopped even occasional use of cannabis by the early 1970s—because he felt it was interfering with his automatic writing exercises. The one substance on which he seemed to have a dependency was Lipton instant iced tea. He drank it con-stantly, with tap water, no sugar, no ice.

Nights of Naomi was one of the few books of American hard-core surrealism I'd read. By hard-core, I mean blunt-force surrealism, I mean there was nothing *neo*-surreal about it. It was straight from the surrealist manifestos, but entirely his own. The poems are violent, dark, and guttural. I remember Knott telling me at the time that he re-fused to read or write or look at art that wasn't surreal. He was still only twenty-nine or thirty, and surrealism is a young man's game. Only months later, he left fundamentalist surrealism behind but always maintained high levels of unpredictability and verbal (as well as aural) imagination in his poems. He was frequently playful, often with heart-tearing ("as quickly as the rumor of meat / up and down a soup-line"*) insight, and always original.

In the fall of 1973, we were both teaching at Columbia College in Chicago. That Thanksgiving, we were invited by a colleague to share dinner with her family and a few others. Just before the turkey arrived, Bill excused himself from the table. The host waited for him to return before he started carving. Bill didn't return. A few days later, I went to his place and asked him what happened, why did he leave? He said it was too painful for him to be in a warm family situation.

In early 1974, Barn Dream Press published another book of Knott's: *Love Poems to Myself*. The title isn't narcissistic: The love poems in the book are dedicated to women he loved. Patrick Botacchi, another college friend, also in the printing trade, joined our publishing venture. *Love Poems to Myself* was printed offset but was still very handsome. It had a striking four-color cover, which was very rare in those days for a small press. When Knott first saw this book, he didn't toss it over his shoulder. Instead, he got a legal aid lawyer and attempted to sue us. I'd said to him in a letter that we'd use a painting by a very good painter, his girlfriend at the time, on the cover. Due to a miscommunication, Barn Dream used another design. Nothing came of this lawsuit. Knott told me later that the lawyer had said: "Sue them for what?" A few times, when I'd run across the book, particularly in the Boston/Cambridge area, the covers were torn off. I don't remember this inci-

*From an uncollected poem.

dent changing our friendship. I saw him very frequently in these years—in Boston/Cambridge, Ohio, Chicago, Iowa, New York, at the MacDowell Colony. We corresponded regularly.

I've spoken of Bill's eccentricities, even some mistakes he made. I haven't gone into any analytical reasons for why I love his poems. The words "analytical" and "love" seem incompatible to me. I haven't said much about why I loved him, the man. I want to make it clear that his idiosyncrasies and even his suffering made up only a small part of the man I knew. In my opinion, Knott did not become an exceptional poet because he was an orphan, because of abuse, because of poverty, because of illness, because of any kind of suffering. *Everybody* suffers. Knott became an exceptional poet despite those things.

Bill Knott is a quintessential, almost primal lyric poet, primal in the sense that his poems seem to emerge from his bone marrow as well as from his heart and mind. He follows an ancient poetic pulse and impulse: The poem, especially the lyric poem, and even more so the sonnet, "is a small vessel that takes a turn a little over halfway down."* Knott possessed a wide range of subject matter, a long working life, and a prodigious work ethic.

In the late 1970s (we were on a subway in New York City, going uptown) he showed me a notebook that was filled, over and over, with different variations on two lines that later showed up in his great poem "The Closet." I wish I could remember which two lines, but I can't.

He approached poems from many different angles and was (see above) a relentless rewriter. Once in a while, I think, he *over*-distilled certain poems. His humor is often biting—and bitten, self-deprecating,

*Edward Hirsch, *A Poet's Glossary* (New York: Houghton Mifflin Harcourt, 2014), p. 593.

self-denigrating, self-abnegating; darkly, darkly so, sometimes. But he also can be flat-out funny. I mean laugh-out-loud funny. He was a hard-core, card-carrying surrealist, a poet of stunning lyric tenderness, and he was a brilliant and innovatively traditional metricist. Sometimes all three at once.

You will find many sonnets of many kinds in this book. There are also dozens of other examples of traditional craftsmanship. Like all good artists, he learned the rules before he began to bend and break them. Knott is a deeply American poet (he came from the heartland and returned there in his last years), but he loved to quote W. B. Yeats's famous exhortation, "Irish poets, learn your trade / sing whatever is well made." I heard him say many times: "Poetry is an art form, poetry is a craft."

He loathed clichés. He disdained preciousness. As dense as some of his poems can be, they rarely defeat comprehensibility. Some are so lucid and straightforward, they are like a punch in the gut, or one's first great kiss. There are poems in syllabics, in various rhyme schemes; and the longest poem in the book, about ten pages, is in seven-syllable lines of full- and half-rhymed couplets. In his so-called free verse poems, Knott pays fierce attention to pacing, diction, tone, syntax, line breaks. And always: noises, sonics, music, *sounds*. He agreed with Robert Frost: "Words exist in the mouth not in books." His intense focus on every syllable, and the sound of every syllable in relation to nearby sounds, is so skilled that the poems often seem casual: Art hides art. He writes for the voice and the page, equally.

As Thomas Wentworth Higginson said after reading some of Emily Dickinson's poems, "When a thought takes one's breath away, who cares to count the syllables?" Poems in this book will take your breath away, providing you have breath when you read them. Something

Knott shares with Dickinson is a sense of compression, distillation, of trying, always, to make more happen with fewer words. He loved her poems fiercely and those, too, I think for similar reasons, of Marina Tsvetaeva, the great Russian poet: for their courage and imagination. Knott's poems think in images, in the "higher algebra"* of metaphor. He loads his poems (see "Every Rift with Ore," page 26). His imagination is relentlessly poetic. He loved Paul Valéry's supposed response to the question of why he didn't write prose: "Because I cannot stand the idea of writing a line like 'And then Madam put on her hat and walked out the door.'"

Knott often favors highly accented language ("old woe clothes") and compound words ("shroudmeal"). Gerard Manley Hopkins wrote: "Stress is the life of it." Knott loves play and puns that express mischief and/or satire ("Rilkemilky," "gangplanking," "mal-de-mess," "immallarméan"). He liked neologisms and semi-neologisms. He is not averse to using a noun, such as "precipice," as a verb. Scientists now tell us this kind of verbal surprise causes little explosions in our brains. He liked, sometimes, to make the reader hear two words in one word, and to make both work in context.

Knott can be outraged (and outrageous), "thorny,"† original, accessible, electrical, occasionally impolite, and heartbreaking. His love poems are exquisite.

Hundreds of *lines*, if lifted from Knott's poems, can stand, or almost stand, as poems by themselves. In fact, there are several one-line poems in this book and even a huge *two-word* poem (three, if you count the title).

*Quote from Ortega y Gasset.
†Robert Pinsky called Knott a "thorny genius" in *The Washington Post* (online) on April 17, 2005.

In all these crossings, these vectors, Knott's high imagination, great skills, singular music, and crazy-beautiful heart meet and often result in unforgettable collisions.

As perpetually insolvent as he was in the years described earlier, Bill was also incredibly generous. One year (1979?), he got an NEA grant and gave me $1,000 (I didn't ask) because he knew I was broke. Although he was never a classroom teacher of mine, I learned more about poetry from him than from anyone I've ever known. He had read all of English and American poetry. I'm tempted to say, *twice.* He'd recite from Wordsworth or Shelley and many others as long as you let him. He was more familiar with foreign poets in translation than anyone else I knew. I remember him mock-raving about the above-mentioned Marina Tsvetaeva on a bus in Chicago. He was outraged that her poems were so hard to find in English. Other passengers seemed unconcerned.

His deep admiration for the poetry of others is what helped him endure and continue to write so well, despite worsening health problems, to his own exacting standards, into his seventies. See "Poem in the Cardiac Unit" on pages 198–99.

If someone ever does a concordance of Knott's work, I predict that his two favorite words will be "clone," as a noun or verb, and "pore" or "pores," as in those little entrances and exits in our skin. I loved his laugh: a kind of chortle, never too loud, unguarded. He never lost his flat Midwestern accent. His hands were beautiful. At least two different women told me this, and one compared his hands to those of John Donne in the anonymous portrait found on the cover of many of his collections.

Knott published twelve print books between 1968 and 2004—with small presses, university presses, and major houses. Sometime around 2005, he decided to forgo traditional print publishing and put all his poems online, for free. He also published many books through Amazon.com and sold them for the price of printing and mailing.

Bill Knott could be the embodiment of the Groucho Marx joke about not wanting to be in a club that allowed members like him. With Bill, however, it wasn't a joke. I saw in him, most often, a kindness, an acute mindfulness of others, even a sweetness, much more than I saw anger, or withdrawal, or rudeness. Was he contradictory? All right then, he was contradictory.

I believe Bill Knott stood out in the rain and was struck by lightning at least the dozen or two dozen times to qualify (using Randall Jarrell's formula/metaphor) as a great poet. He is one, in a school of one, among the American poets. I believe this will become more and more evident, maybe even obvious (if these kinds of things continue to matter in our culture), as the decades, like barges, keep moving toward the sea.

THOMAS LUX

ATLANTA

DECEMBER 2015

×××

I took almost all the poems in this volume from a book Bill Knott published through Amazon.com called *Collected Poetry 1960–2014*. It is dated, on the cover, 02/24/14, less than three weeks before he died. There are 964 poems in that collection; 152 poems are in this volume. I added five poems that were not in the *Collected*. Since he did not include any poems from *Nights of Naomi* in the *Collected*, I did not include any here. I also kept, with a few minor exceptions, the progression of his order, which he said "is meant to be random, neither chronological nor thematic, though I may have failed to achieve that intention in all instances."

I AM FLYING INTO MYSELF

GOODBYE

If you are still alive when you read this,
close your eyes. I am
under their lids, growing black.

TO A DEAD FRIEND

mourning clothes worn
inside out
would be white
if things were right
if opposites ruled

if truth prevailed
then me and you
would be two
instead of the one
we've become

THE GOLDEN AGE

is thought to be a confession, won by endless
torture, but which our interrogators must
hate to record—all those old code names, dates,
the standard narrative of sandpaper
throats, even their remorse, fall ignored. Far

away, a late (not lost) messenger stares,
struck by window bargains or is it the gift
of a sudden solicitude: is she going to
lift up her shadow's weight, shift hers
onto it? She knows who bears whom. In

that momentary museum where memory occurs,
more accrue of those torturers' pincers than
lessened fingernails, eyes teased to a pulp,
we beg for closeups. *Ormolus, objets d'art!*
A satyr drains an hourglass with one gulp.

POEM

I first loved you
Second to your gentleness

Like the blind who
Divide their lives into
Dark and dark I
Have you and your gentleness

As a detail in a painting frames that painting
In the often
Memory, your face
Is surrounded by your eyes
Unafraid
Of the grays of gentleness

But better than your gentleness
I love your harshness
When you talk about that prison capitalism
When you vow never to stop fighting

Never

Until each woman and man is free

Until each woman and man is in the custody

Of their gentleness

OPERATION CROSSZERO

Sunny or storm the clouds always once
Will form some sudden shape which appears
Unique, though may that same shadowstance
Recur each thirty-three point three years?

Shall heaven's cycles of beginnings
And ends hover concealed from the eye:
What blitzkrieg visits have its big bangs
Planned; whose planet-kills queue that blue sky.

Their blast orbits blind deciphersight—
Or can reconnaissance flights thrust up
Agents to infiltrate that great height,
Stealth probes properly trained to snoop deep.

On earth secrets beget enemies . . .
Clandestine torture, covert sortie—
Let's intell-strip bare those star countries.
A third of the way through his thirty

Third year we hoisted up our best black
Op to spydrop us down more data;
The turncoat never reported back,
(Codename: Christ) the dirty traitor.

PARABLE FROM CHILDHOOD

Something about a pond, and on the pond
a paper boat; something about a child's
act, dropping a pebble upon that boat
to study the effect: but then to let
other pebbles fall to see if it holds,
to kneel there spilling them one after one
until, until finally . . . If I weigh
this poem down with much more, it too will sink—

Writing my poems of a boy on the brink
has shown how ripples horizoned by sky
remain the only real cargo aboard
whatever that craft that unmoored us was,
and yet why he treasured such passages.
Saying they be lost we would launch each word.

ADVICE FROM THE EXPERTS

I lay down in the empty street and parked
My feet against the gutter's curb while from
The building above a bunch of gawkers perched
Along its ledges urged me don't, don't jump.

HISTORY

Hope . . . goosestep.

THE UNSUBSCRIBER

Like all children, you were a de facto
Member of the Flat Earth Society,
Believing nothing but what you could see
Or touch or whatever sense led act to

Fruition: mudpies made summer beneath
A tree whose measured shade endowed decrees
Between light and dark: such hierarchies
Gave you implicit, a sophistic faith—

(Fallacious fellowship!)— Youth's adherents
Ignore the fact that most factions reject
Their lyric league (which only fools have stayed

Striplings of) and none condone its nonsense:
No one loves that vain solipsistic sect
You'd never join, whose dues you've always paid.

FIRST SIGHT

Summer is entered through screendoors,
and therefore seems unclear
at first sight, when it is in fact
a mesh of fine wires
suspended panewise
whose haze has confused the eyes . . .

What if we never entered then—
what if the days remained like this,
a hesitation at the threshold of itself,
expectant, tense, tensile
as lines that crisscross each other
in a space forever latent
where we wait, pressed up against
something trying to retain its vagueness.

PLUNGE

at night one drop of rain
falls from each star
as if it were being lowered
on a string

and yet that storm of plummets
is never enough
to wet any of the planets
that pass through it

only the blackness the space
between us is washed
away by these singular
lettings-down of water

distance is washed away
all the worlds merge
for a liquid moment
our island eyes

and suddenly we understand
why umbrellas love
to dive
into clouds

STRAND

To swim in water colored green
means you may never reach the shore—
but if the waves are blue, then you
might retrieve your stroke and strike more.

Past surface shades could find the one
arranging dust, the hue your own
adequately echoes, earth tone.

Neither primary nor pastel,
its prism all but shallow bathes
every island that can be found
in scenes preserved in paint: it saves

the picturesque yet quickly drowns
our honed harbor, your wake, your wake
says, flowing home beneath no ground.

BY THE RIVER BAAB

We know that somewhere far north of here
the two rivers Ba and Ab converge to form
this greater stream that sustains us, uniting
the lifeblood length of our lands: and we believe
that the Ba's source is heaven, the Ab's hell.

Daily expeditions embark upcountry to find
that fork, to learn where the merge first occurs.
Too far: none of our explorers return. Or
else when they reach that point they themselves
are torn apart by a sudden urge to choose—

to resolutely take either the Ba/the Ab, and trace
good or evil to its spring. Each flips a coin
perhaps, or favors whichever one the wind's
blowing from at that moment. Down here
even we who have not the heart to venture

anywhere that would force us to such deep
decisions, even we, when we hold that glass of
water in our hand, drink it slowly, deliberately,
as if we could taste the two strains, could somehow
distinguish their twin flow through our veins.

SUNSET AND NOON: MARJORY P.

Each face strikes a different hour in the heart
The final tolling it will be yours
(Its profile's panels on which are sleep-lacquered-eye
The golden flights and returns of an unblemished wound)

Like a blind person reading smoke signals, I touch
The face foretold as yours
(It's like a boney honey in the sunset, pale laughter of
    leeches, a teardrop (that Rosetta Pebble leading to the
    eventual decipherments of all things in the sky: sunset
    and noon) and if you've started thinking about now
    that this is a long line you're wrong cause this is no
    line this is a caress and it won't stop until it reaches
    your smile of permanent collisions)
Pale laughter of leeches, the still-unblemished wound

Then to rise by noon when the horizon's tug-of-war is raging
To sink by noon in a white studio embracing
—The sky directionless as children who keep getting
    kissed on top their heads
They turn thus way and that, dizzy, mad.

BAD HABIT

At least once a day,
every day,
to ensure that my facial
compatibility with God's is nil,
I smile.

RIGOR VITUS

I walk
On human stilts.
To my right lower leg a man is locked rigid;
To the left a woman, lifelessly strapped.

I have to heave them up,
Heft them out and but they're so heavy (heavy as head)
Seems all my strength
Just take the begin step—

All my past to broach a future. And on top of that,
They're not even dead,
Those ol' hypocrites.
They perk up when they want to, they please and pleasure themselves,

It's terrible. The one consolation:
When they make love,
To someone who's far or close enough away appears it appears then
Like I'm dancing.

Painting is a person placed
between the light and a
canvas so that their shadow
is cast on the canvas and
then the person signs their
name on it whereas poetry
is the shadow writing its
name upon the person.

DEATH

Going to sleep, I cross my hands on my chest.
They will place my hands like this.
It will look as though I am flying into myself.

POEM (HOW I LOST MY PEN-NAME)

I wrote under a pen-name
One day I shook the pen trying to make the name come out
But no it's
Like me prefers clinging to the inner calypso

So I tossed the pen to my pet the
Wastebasket to eat
It'll vomit back the name
Names aren't fit
For unhuman consumption

But no again

It stayed down

I don't use a pen-name anymore
I don't use a pen anymore
I don't write anymore
I just sit looking at the wastebasket
With this alert intelligent look on my face

SECURITY

If I had a magic carpet
I'd keep it
Floating always
Right in front of me
Perpendicular, like a door.

HUMIDITY'S TONES

Four AM, nothing moving, no hurry,
dawn still has time to be choosy
selecting its pinks. But now a breeze
brushes across me—the way my skin
is cooled off by the evaporation
of sweat, this artistry, this system
sombers me: when I am blown from
the body of life will it be refreshed?
I dread the color of the answer Yes.

It's too complex to explain,
but I was already in
the orphanage when dad died;
and so that day when I cried,
to keep the other children safe
from my infectious grief
they left me in lockdown
in some office where I found
piles of comicbooks hid
which they had confiscated
from us kids through the years,
and on through wiped tears
I pored quickly knowing
this was a one-time thing—
this quarantine would soon end—
I'd never see them again:
I'd regret each missed issue,
and worse than that I knew
that if a day ever did come
when I could obtain them,
gee, I'd be too old to read
them then, I'd be like him, dad.

EVERY RIFT WITH ORE

How fiercely foilsome the facial knife shivs
its two blades up to where the forehead ends
as wound-deep-wedged widow's-peaks: how weakly
the old hero hair-line fights back and fends,
each pass of day fewer gray strands save me—
how deadly dull's the duel our sword lives.

MY RIVER

The closer it gets to the sea the more
it aches for its source, the wound
that sprung it from the ground.

TO THE EMBLEMATIC HOURGLASS

OF MY FATHER'S SKULL

The night that dies in me each day is yours:
Hour whose way I stare, yearning to terra
Firma my eye. There. Where a single hair
Would be a theater curtain I could cling

Behind, dreading my cue, aching to hear
What co-hurrah. More, more of leaves that fall
Consummate capsules, having annaled all
Their veins said! Printout printemps. And yet

(Altars our blood writes a blurb for god on)
Can one ever envy enough his skeleton's
Celebrity. Can any epitaph

Be adequate repartee for your laugh.
Days lived by me each night say less than it.
While sleep in ounces weighs me wanting.

ALFONSINA STORNI

Feeling as you wrote that the cancer quote
Is on its way upstairs   to the throat
One breast had already flown   migrant
Heart   de facto amazon   only the sea remained

Like a jealous mattress an   old pillow stuffed
With insomnia's phonebills the sea
Is there to throw oneself at   at dawn   late
Up all night over   a poem called Voy a

Dormir and which says   this   better than this
(Each time I read one by you I revise
Myself my suicide is   to be me instead of you)

Sea that swallowed your poet   throat
Does not   for the having of it   sing less
And besides   only that cancer tried to float

THE SUMMONING

You know your name
Seems to contain
More syllables in
All other mouths
Than mine I hear
I hear these voices
Everywhere the
Waves coming ashore
Add long a's
As they say it
Then sometimes the wind
Puts an o in
The middle and
Babybirds their
Bottomlessness fills
It with e
Whenever I hear it
Screeched
Moaned
Sighed by these things
By everything
I must stop and listen
To my lips
Vehemently

Vainly correcting

The whole world's

Mispronunciations

As if those

Mispronunciations

Were the reason

You were not answering

As if they

Were the reason you

Were not here

Beside me and

My saying it right

My getting it exact

Is all it would take

To call you back.

Pinkie Brown must marry Rose Wilson
to keep her mouth shut about the murder
which the cops don't know wasn't no accident —

Pinkie has a straight razor for slashing,
a vial of acid for throwing into,
a snitch's face. He dies in the end. The end

of the book, I mean — where, on the last page,
"Young Rose" hurries out of church to pray
that her Pinkie has left her preggy-poo . . .

Now, this kid — if he was ever born — joined
a skiffle group in '62 called Brighton
Rockers, didn't make it big, though,

just local dances and do's. Rose,
pink, brown, all nonelemental colors, shades
of shame, melancholy, colors which, you

get caught loving too much, you get sent up
to do time — time, that crime you didn't,
couldn't commit! even if you weren't

born—even and if your dad he died with
that sneer—unsmooched his punk's pure soul, unsaved—
Every Sunday now in church Rose slices

her ring-finger off, onto the collection-plate;
once the sextons have gathered enough
bodily parts from the congregation, enough

to add up to an entire being, the priest sub-
stitutes that entire being for the one
on the cross: they bring Him down in the name

of brown and rose and pink, sadness
and shame, His body, remade, is yelled at
and made to get a haircut, go to school,

study, to do each day like the rest
of us crawling through this igloo of hell,
and laugh it up, show pain a good time,

and read *Brighton Rock* by Graham Greene.

OVERNIGHT FREEZE (HEPTASYLLABICS)

Window-glints of ice glaze fast
what last night flashed the mudflats,

down in which dawn has found pressed
small animal tracks: inch-niched

skylights affix these quick paths—
Each step is trapped beneath slats

of translucency attached
rime to rim: they sit there ditched,

puttied into glare hatches—
All around the ground looks patched

and spattered with puddle-thatch,
but note rather this etched stretch

where a late trotter's tread's latched
with pondgild on its ledge trench:

how glitter-together cached;
incandescently encased.

Not bins or barns' coiled harvest,
glozen molds hold placed this trace,

bold encroachments caught across:
each hoof-, paw-, claw-mark's embossed

by its lunge run: each rut crests
to extend its range, end-launched—

it must hate these lit nimbus
lids, must wince beneath such frost—

sun has tamed them flame of squints
yet some after-image haunts:

Lands on every side lie creased
with spoor that mars their hard crust

and floorflares most summer's waste
imagination, that pinch

not worth pittance, that thin purse
clutching what breast abundance

of flurry foliage tossed, prize
profligate with years' penance

whose cease has summoned what peace—
tarp white winter's carapace

tries to hide that mislaid dust
carrion in granaries

and bury deeper what grace
war's warrior deifies—

what Troy, what toy's sacrifice
leaks justification, beast

whose Homered oathswraths can't match
this farmstead's secular crafts—

Beyond the coop's chickenhatch
pieces of a greenhouse burst

up from the clays as ghosts pass
to implant sole-sills for what's

still clear to me—I approach
each glimpsy-glaziered gapgulch

afraid my galoshes squelch
break their skittery sketches

or skidheel slide a childprance
puncturing every damn sash

I can smash, whatever blanched
and specious glow my outstanced

kick can dislodge idolfest
haloes those pit-portholes hoist

from lamb-trample slaughterous
gods displayed bad raptor hosts—

herds of ape they pasture-traipse
bestial cattlecats who scratch

paved prowess in the dirt splotch
like border-dots on mapwatch

or liens miser ledgers clutch
feral figures for our debts

predator prey pays poets
that panther pads our wallets

Ted Hughes' cunning hawk-pastiche
plugs its parrot author rich

this savage extravagance
animates each TV pitch

breakfast lions and leopets
mad advertiser rabbits

like easter eggs and christ crèche
exist to rake in the cash

as you sit and clicker switch
from Tiger Attack stabsites

to Martyred Bible Prophets
can you diff any difference

in sanguinary scams which
verse-ho's popes and other shits

exchange/exploit for lootsplits
getcher *guts* getcher *spirits*

festering fetish lame wish
goldgash wildpack "religious"

imperious dazzlements
its screen between me unleashed

shall I plain idealize
the sight. Pitter-pattered glitz

the poorest field-rat can task:
"Trance entombed, my forage-struts?

strangely crowned with iciclets,
thaw-askance in silver nets

that snag some Nixnaut banished
from huge spook-lakes diminished

to these mini: spangle-splashed
and scaly his mermarsh face

is damming yours to a drowse:
your powers sod, your earth cursed,

bear null this lair's fatal laze—
bide its nether-tide enclosed,

its potent emptiness poised
to bolt free, vain, hopeless wish:

train of hymen's bridal dress,
heil flower drowned mire and mess

in this fecal foul recess—
delusional any parse

that aspires to soar from smutch
or scat escape its burnished,

prison-urned prism-units
lathed and locked, crystal cubits

where spate-carpeted carets—
pools, flood-scummed with gem, facets

unstrung-flung diamond pendants
it strangles you, chain necklaced.

Immured your murder-led bents
that followed friendly bloodscents

till fangs throat-fonts firmly drenched
and feast fell anticlimax—

till: cycle lay established,
again. Eternal matrix,

your game's destined accidents
choreograph each pounce once

but here they're preserved in twice:
cryocrypts halt their advance,

vaults for phantom enpassants—
stabatjammed their rhythm dance.

Here stands this clearing's essence,
filmed upon fillspace distance—

oh hear its car-crash score-scants:
sharkshrieks stilled, prowl-growls silenced.

Look: its slope grows near scar grazed
with overtook veer. Fear-crazed

leap-lopes, laned below this sluice
raid, rapacious avalanche—

this meander labyrinth's
constellated your hunt-sprints.

Star-quenched in lurid casements
what vent revives these vagrants.

Plunged in pent, your harms unhitched.
Sprawled for sleep's random ambush—

hibernate, die! sink finished
along this blank fishtank maze

or wake, with mindblink ablaze—
see your scintillant depths catch

magic from the mimic glance
of this mirror while it lasts—

how soon noon will melt to mush
your hoar hour which Eskimos

have more words for than I, mouse
Michigander, verminous

mite of this sheer terminus
the Knott brat teetertoes his

trespass at. He has spare choice
and careless proceed he must

toward the devouring bless
this coldsnap moment's incised

in his own flesh. Oedipus
ankled. Pale autumn's glozes

grail incarnation of slush
frail trail we fugitives mashed

in the wet soil till chill lashed
in tight with glacier paces

palls in the mornings' stale mess
of luminescence. Sunrise

et al. Against its bright best
(nature's norm-channel brilliance

versus some thumbed thesaurus)
this polar-stamped dirt contrasts

my feet in a fret of froze
silly syllabic sets of rows

extinguished glimmer glimpses
shattered all their gleams I guess—"

Stoic, lone, those shine-lines cast
to show no magnificence

or quests quixotic-thrust, just
folk stalked by their hungriness,

critters croaked, varmints vanished
species extinct or deathwish—

Theirs is not an innocence
chosen, their hands are not clenched

on church-prayers' lack-response.
Their trek unlike ours abounds.

Under gait-grates it waits wise
in its ways portrayed saycheese—

Carnivore, killer-corps seized;
poacher captured, frozenchase.

Mid-stride taken, frigid paste
haste-hail jails this trodden caste.

Roadcage for an arctic race;
shod-zoo stocked with dull dreambrates.

Before the snow's blind expanse
blunders every further fence

a walk may stop precipice
top this fierce fenestrate lens

but what happens then depends
on some lost, glossed-over sense.

One might pause to muse that post
or else forget, astonished.

Or kneel to urge weathers worse
come seal his brr-brief life's course—

(Let elf and unicorn dash
climate at its timeliest

congeals their furtive crevasse
strayhorde stayed for a nor' rest.)

Spurts of rhyme, "spots of time," sparse
for suicide-sake. Because

it all seems so colorless.
The past and everything since.

But our chameleon's footprints—
have they been paned with stained glass?

GOING MY WAY

The one boy who died of polio
in our orphanage in the early
1950s was such an important
icon that even now I remember
his favorite movie since that's
what we do with the famous,
retain some anomalous fact
that quiets them in our mind.
We, I say, but was it everyone—
did all of us shed that kid: did
a thousand child incarcerates
replace his face-and-name with
an actor's mask and cast it as
star of the waste disease whose
cause was always doubt, germ
caught perhaps from local lakes
prohibited. Who thought of him
those summers we could not
swim until a vaccine came, too
late to amend lackwarm days,
to change our fate/our film to his.
That movie—*Going My Way*
featuring Bing Crosby as a young
priest, kindly, loveable, unreal—

Tommy, Jimmy, whatever he
was called, he probably knows
still by still now every camera
angle and closeup, every cut
we living are allowed to forget.

ELEMENTARY LESSON

Sometimes even in Math class a downpour
Would rise against the windows and render
The normal decorum hard to restore—
Fittingly we'd split a grin when lightning
Stuck out its multiple tongue at teacher.

Smartlike fling our arms in the air, crying
To be called on, smug, eye-bright, cheek-aware
When thunder drowns our correctest answer.
A failsafe secret form of defying.
(Not like spitballing the hall monitor.)

These quickstorms were at last the world's Recess,
Whose games toss random nebu-numerals
In play impromptu streams and teams across
Unmarked-off endless fields or else more schools
Reluctant-ruled, would-be truants like us—

Just our luck those heavenstruck distractions
From final test results grow dull and show
As adults—these afteryears—their brilliant
Fractiousness scores less than quantic fractions.
Most of childhood's coups come to sum zero.

Despite which some delinquencies linger—
Take our instinctive counting by finger—
(All other tallies seem cramped in compare)—
Since age equals memory times failure—
Though mentor modes slam such bad behavior:

Our worst, they swear, is using metaphor
To avoid the quiz/to solve the problem.
Leaners from lecterns omniforum warn
That effing mistake is what makes us dumb.
Minusminds, try to amend your error.

Those tutors tell us still—they always will—
Go suffer fools what all erasers learn,
To rain down wrong as good—they talk and talk!
But in the meanwhile: cloud loud as a chalk
Rattling back in rack on the blackboard's sill.

(THE PUNCH AND JUDY)

People who get down on their knees to me are the answer
    to my prayers
You said
I said
The fortuneteller said

Masturbate onto the table
I will read your semen
These patterns are constellations
To a dare

Devil sleeper all night
I cried
You said

Free me or worship me
Descended
Like curtains that cut puppeteers' hands off

FROM AN OLD LEGEND

let's cut some graftings
from off these trees and
uproot those hedgerows
and hold their foliage go
armed with camouflage as
we approach the castle
hoping they won't notice
our smirks and winks
our shining eyes maybe
leafsecreted we can plant
quick shrubs and shoots
around its impregnable
walls then waltz away leaving
their fortress enforested

THE CLOSET

(. . . after my mother's death)

Here not long enough after the hospital happened
I find her closet lying empty and stop my play
And go in and crane up at three blackwire hangers
Which quiver, airy, released. They appear to enjoy

Their new distance, cognizance born of the absence
Of anything else. The closet has been cleaned out
Full-flush as surgeries where the hangers could be
Amiable scalpels though they just as well would be

Themselves, in basements, glovelessly scraping uteri
But, here, pure, transfigured heavenward, they're
Birds, whose wingspans expand by excluding me. Their
Range is enlarged by loss. They'd leave buzzards

Measly as moths: and the hatshelf is even higher!
As the sky over a prairie, an undotted desert where
Nothing can swoop sudden, crumple in secret. I've fled
At ambush, tag, age: six, must I face this, can

I have my hide-and-seek hole back now please, the
Clothes, the thicket of shoes, where is it? Only
The hangers are at home here. Come heir to this
Rare element, fluent, their skeletal grace sings

Of the ease with which they let go the dress, slip,
Housecoat or blouse, so absolvingly. Free, they fly
Trim, triangular, augurs leapt ahead from some geometric
God who soars stripped (of flesh, it is said): catnip

To a brat placated by model airplane kits kids
My size lack motorskills for, I wind up all glue-scabbed,
Pawing goo-goo fingernails, glaze skins fun to peer in as
Frost-i-glass doors . . . But the closet has no windows.

Opaque or sheer: I must shut my eyes, shrink within
To peep into this wall. Soliciting sleep I'll dream
Mother spilled and cold, unpillowed, the operating-
Table cracked to goad delivery: its stirrups slack,

Its forceps closed: by it I'll see mobs of obstetrical
Personnel kneel proud, congratulatory, cooing
And oohing and hold the dead infant up to the dead
Woman's face as if for approval, the prompted

Beholding, tears, a zoomshot kiss. White-masked
Doctors and nurses patting each other on the back,
Which is how in the Old West a hangman, if
He was good, could gauge the heft of his intended . . .

Awake, the hangers are sharper, knife-'n'-slice, I jump
Helplessly to catch them to twist them clear,
Mis-shape them whole, sail them across the small air
Space of the closet. I shall find room enough here

By excluding myself; by excluding myself, I'll grow.

MRS. FRYE AND THE PENCILSHARPENER

I'll remember how in 8th-grade English class, always
bending toward the desk I would try to avert my eyes
from the mysterious ways Mrs. Frye's hair displaced
the blackboard's space with its black coils, to the paper
my penciltip raced across, certain to pass each test:
and if these gaze shifts got too switcheroo I'd retreat
(daily, it seems) to the back of the packed classroom

where, leaning forward on my toes, I could push with
my left hand the nubile tube of wood into the mouth
of the pencilsharpener which hung there like some
natural protrusion of the wall, an indigenous Deity,
the mask of a Goddess, erosion-endowed, rockformed—
then feel my righthand fingers and thumb slowly turn
the oiled wheel while knowing I would have to face

close to that sac-shaped sharpener, have to inhale
the high smell of its depths, earthy, ripe, pubic: to see
in my mind the pairings inside, those musky dark curls
whose incense was increased of course like mold-mildew
by the subtle saliva we kids might use to lick the lead's
point, though nearly none of our tongues could unblunt
the conundrums grownups posed, in my case Mrs. Frye

especially: so if I lingered back there, grinding away,
it was not to gloat, not to play the saintly A-student
snickering from behind at the others' heads bent intent
as penitents, because I too, I sinned at times, whenas,
no matter how proud I was of my proper grammar or
propounded syntax, stuffing my text thick with fetish
parsemarks, I myself went taunted, teased by the urge

to erase the very prodigy evidence my page revealed—
all the knots and quirks of those perfectly traced letters—
to restore the blankness I spoiled with each sentence—
to castrate every phrase before its errors rose by rote
to make my cthonic-greatest mistake grow and grow
erectile, inherent, that habit hateful male participle
I always was unable to shear the nib the stuff off of—

*

(But how could I flub and flunk such a crucial ordeal?—
Forgive me: I was lost pondering, musing about a poem
memorized from the boys' bathroom, tongued fluent
but not understood: yet how truthshod its lines ran
to my anxiety—their meaning escaped the precocious,
the goldstar me—so if I stalled—if I stayed chewed over
and left a stammering dimwit by their immallarméan

import, which paired its print alongside a syllabus
of pornocoiled stick figures whose mouths were pierced
by the sharpened ends of toonballoons—verses verse
alone can't explicate in systematic prosaic terms that

forced and torsoed my head shy—if I was stuck on
their sphinxian simplicity—unable to decipher any
of the prodigal doggerel lessons gesticulated down

our school's scribbly corridors, snicked and snatched at
across its game fields, a whole curriculum of secret lore,
a litany of my-big-brother-told-me's, my-uncle-said's,
a rumor primer which claimed complete mastery of
the only discipline impenetrable to my inquisitive
quests never mind the autodidact airs I had to affect
during discussions of this topic, the nods and knowing

grins I wore to pass, to show my mastery of its arcana,
to prove what a pored nerd drill-diligent pupil I was
of those endless piss-walls, those scrawled rhymes and
confident lectures by croneys and guys who made sense
of the insane instructions re the sole subject I mark
zero on: all the dunno-dumb ideas I dunned then drove
core to me, carved their myths into me—and one in

particular goes to this poem, from the gendergabble
that gorged my brain: it hissed that She/the unknown
reared an inward toothly sheathdeath essence geared
to vagina dentata whatever pedant-pendant I'd proffer,
I, alma-matered to cram every exam with phallocratic
tits and sexist tripe pseudotype scionbabble, the entire
wisdom of my mentors' art-patriarch, old gobbledy-tropes—)

*

All gradeschool the fear of failing hovered in overstudy
as children riddled ears never to be learned, but could
I have continued to hone my fate, could I have stood
there for years and still the pencilsharpener wait
like a patient questioner, a warm, smiling teacher,
filled with such dense scents, shavings, shorn graphite,
its soil rich with words no one would ever have to write.

KNOT (HENDECASYLLABICS)

After you've sewn it, bite the thread off my grave —
Please leave no loose seam of me to wave above
The bones unknitting, the flesh unweaving love.

MY MOTHER'S LIST OF NAMES

My mother's list of names today I take it in my hand
And read the places she underlined William and Ann
The others are my brothers and sisters I know
I'm going to see them when I'm fully grown

Yes they're waiting for me to join 'em and I will
Just over the top of that great big hill
Lies a green valley where their shouts of joy are fellowing
Save all but one can be seen there next a kin

And a link is missing from their ringarosey dance
Think of the names she wrote down not just by chance
When she learned that a baby inside her was growing small
She placed that list inside the family Bible

Then I was born and she died soon after
And I grew up sinful of questions I could not ask her
I did not know she had left me the answer
Pressed between the holy pages with the happy laughter
Of John, Rudolph, Frank, Arthur, Paul,
Pauline, Martha, Ann, Doris, Susan, you all,

I did not know you were even alive
Till I read the Bible today for the first time in my life
And found this list of names that might have been my own
You other me's on the bright side of my moon

Mother and Daddy too have joined you in play
And I am coming to complete the circle of your day
I was a lonely child I never understood that you
Were waiting for me to find the truth and know

And I'll make this one promise you want me to:
I'm goin' to continue my Bible study
Till I'm back in the body
With you.

GREEN-HEED

The grass on my mother's grave
is a sparse species which must have

yearly tearfalls from at least
one mourner to merely subsist;

there are verses where lament
rains forth a veritable font:

compared with their cataract
whatever moisture mine may lack

shall always wither in drought
seed-deep as her greedy grief-root;

whose weed needs the kind of care
I should spare no shame to shed here.

Perhaps there are more eyes who've cried
than I feel dried up inside.

TRUE STORY

We stole the rich couple's baby
and left our own infant with
a note demanding they raise our
child as if it were theirs and we

would do the same. Signed,
A Poor Couple. Decades later
our son racks summa cum laude
while theirs drapes our hovel

with beercans. But did we prove
our point? This heroic experiment
(a jeu de joie of performance art)

attempts to assert the adroit
of nurture over nature, the pure
narrative we write in order to write.

PEACE (PASCAL)

There is a valley
Is the oldest story.

Its temperature qualities
Make us descend the trees
To settle down beside
Fruits and fields.

By its river content
To sit quietly in a small tent
To fashion fishing spears
From fallen limbs.

No need to climb its hills
No need to go up there
To look to see
Another valley.

ISLANDS

Garden hoses on horseback
gallop through the desert
to fill up the gulfs
that surround us.

Born of the birds who leave
their eggs on the rim
of volcanoes, then fly off
never to return:
that nursive warmth
erupts us into form.

Lava solidifies the sea
for binoculars of hourly ships
whose cruel captains allow
the stowaway days
no shore, no leave.

But the wisdom of archipelago,
how one must stop sometimes
to meet one's feet
on sites prepared for none.

Over each beach
senior sand and junior dune
establish their shifty dynasty.

Meanwhile look at all the water.

The waves
are swimmers no one saves.

SUITE (TO HOKU)

A poem is a room that contains
the house it's in, the way you
accommodate me when I lie
beside you, even if the address
is lost so many times and the names
of streets are strangers that pass
shuffling a card-deck of maps
whose rubberband has snapped:
still beyond all chance or choice
perhaps, your arms fold mine
to indicate location, the close
custom of place held together
or flung into the bedroom's air
where your dress tries to come in
from the rain it has become:
the way shelter finds us one again,
and the opus of this nearness,
the poem on its own, wandering.

ANT DODGER

A suicide applicant
Who braces himself out
On a high ledge at noon
While busy peeking down

Noticed an ant crawling
Dottily on the ledge
Right
There near his left toe

Below crowds all pushed
Oblivious babbling
Omniscient like in the movies
Out whooshy doors

But his gaze halt ant
Ant the true ant
He dimly remembers
Not like them

So now
He hesitates
A million stories up
Shifts weight trying

Make his mind up
Distantly deciding
Whether to step
Before he jumps

On it
Or not

NIGHT THOUGHT

Compared to one's normal clothes, pajamas
are just as caricature as the dreams
they bare: farce-skins, facades, unserious
film versions of the *mode diem*, they seem
to have come from a posthumousness;
floppy statues of ourselves, slack seams
of death. Their form mimics the decay
that will fit us so comfortably someday.

CHRISTMAS AT THE ORPHANAGE

But if they'd give us toys and twice the stuff
most parents splurge on the average kid,
orphans, I submit, need more than enough;
in fact, stacks wrapped with our names nearly hid
the tree where sparkling allotments yearly
guaranteed a lack of—what?—family?—

I knew exactly what it was I missed:
(did each boy there feel the same denials?)
to share my pals' tearing open their piles
meant sealing the self, the child that wanted
to scream at all You stole those gifts from me;
whose birthday is worth such words? The wish-lists
they'd made us write out in May lay granted
against starred branches. I said I'm sorry.

TO MYSELF

Poetry
can be
the magic
carpet

which you say
you want,
but only
if you

stand willing
to pull
that rug out

from under
your own
feet, daily.

POEM

Your nakedness: the sound when I break an apple in half.

I recently killed my father

And will soon marry my mother;

My question is:

Should his side of the family be invited to the wedding?

QUICKIE

Poetry
is
like
sex
on
quicksand
ergo
foreplay
should
be
kept
at
a
minimum

WIDOW/WIDOWER'S WINTER

Outside, the snow is falling into its past . . .
I do want this night to end.
In the fireplace,
a section of ash caves in.

The fall day you were buried,
birds went over,
south,
thick enough to carry someone.

They took my gapes of breath.
—Their fuel?
We are together in some birds, who fail.

I didn't want to look down, to glimpse your grave,
its heroic little mound
like the peck of dirt we hope to eat in our life.

POEM

On a shroudmeal coast
Freak reefs currents winds
Stands a lighthouse inside
    Steep and stairy

Rooms a keeper on humdrum
Work rounds walks banging
Wax knees slamming
Across scarred chairs for

    Just though eye
Sight's clear and the echo
Calm chamber are
    Warm lit as sharp

    Rocks waves froth out there
Through which harried
Tankers' thanks thread
    High beacon ribs

    Smack into steel
Thermometers a filecase face
Hits mirrors can't help
    It.

Against every
Faucet bed chart table star
Rung transmitter receiver he's
Rolled and tossed.

THE SPELL

All the days with you in them
are better than the ones with I.
If you were me you'd know why.

All the words with o in them
are better than the ones with e.
If you were me you'd see.

Best of all of course is a
because it always comes first, ha!
(Is it better being me or worse.)

But say these charms reversed
at times, would I worry who
surpasses me as versus you—

at times I could barely tell.
Better is good but not as well.

FRAGMENT

Because at least one couple is making love
Somewhere in the world at all times,
Because those two are always pressed tightly together,
Hatred can never slip between them
To come destroy us.

THE D AND M'S

I've got the D and M's,
despondency madness
hare me everywhere,
despair or mal-de-mess.

Diagnosis is malignant,
day channels the moon,
my denials mechanical,
all darkness unders mine.

Dearth and mourn.
Doldrums in mire.
I've got the D and M's

and all their dire malign
deep-plodes my mind.
I can't stand these damns.

DEPOSITIONING

so billions of humans for millennia looked
at the blue sky of a summer day and saw it as
bright until one day the boy Rimbaud looked
and saw that normal shining blue as darkness

and said I have removed from the sky the blue
which is darkness but his saying so did not
result in heaven being stripped bare of blue
to leave only immense endless light and hot

sun nothing but sun from horizon to horizon
eye-encompassing gorging all-point our view
no and in fact and amazingly his sly vision
or petition proved to have been only a sight

true and all despite his deposition the blue
which is darkness stayed it remained bright

EVICTION PROCESS

Wreckball all the highrises:
then use the cornerstones of those
leveled towers to create my castle:
composed solely of foundationstones,
each one of which was blessed
with a ceremony, a literal
groundbreaking and therefore whole;
each block unique,
inscribed with ritual aggrandizements;
each planted solemnly:
each underpin laid as the bedrock
its lesser brothers would rest on:
use only these rootstones to raise
the walls of my eyrie house hideaway
whose forbidding frame will have
no real infrastructure, whose form
will be a spiritual suspension
(cradle crux kernel hub core)
wherein each establishingstone
must cohere solid with the weight
of its having once been named
in salutation as such—but surely
when these maidenstones these
consecratalstones are placed

together to make home my dream
my ideal occupancy, then surely
due to the baseless act
of imagining this acme of architecture
I will never be allowed to live here.

NAOMI POEM

With the toys of your nape
With your skin of mother-of-throe pearls
And your fire-sodden glances
From the sidelong world

We break rivulets off the river and wave them in the air
Remember the world has no experience at being you
We also are loving you for the foreverth time
The light, torn from leaf and cry

Even your shoulders are petty crimes

DEPRESSIONISM

Without any necessity to name it or anything,
I remember this bombcrater before it held a garden.
Once I saw children kneel down there to pray for pardon
At an altar on which a little toll-money rolled laughing.

Swift suedes of evening, night's purple peltdown.
I don't have to invoke the past; it's not required.
I'll just settle here stolid like a stopsign repeating
The word I stand for—sit and let my tired feet hang

Over the lip of this pit-deep garden whose intricate
Vines query up at me. Quiet from the town I can hear
Orphans rattling the gravel on their plates and or

Other faux pas I'm under no order to enumerate,—
Jet-lag of angels, a snake, faintings on summer pavements.
This bombfall failed in its intent: having none, I won't.

ANOTHER FIRST KISS: TO X

A first kiss can occur anywhere: two pairs
Of lips might meet as ingredients for
A cannibal's chowder; or on the shore of
A nightclub at ebb. Preferably the latter—

Though there are no more nightclubs, or cannibals,
As such: I mean the first kiss is passé,
Archaic, obsolete. Pre–Global Village,
It rests in wrinkles, in blinking memories . . .

Ours came in bed, but after we'd undressed;
Preceded by hugs. And so the question
Of using the tongue—that old hesitation—
Didn't apply. We plunged right in. At

Our age you get naked and then you neck,
The opposite of how it was done young.
But the hunger is still there. The thirst
Is like in a bar, when they yell out Last Round.

HAIR POEM

Hair is heaven's water flowing eerily over us
Often a woman drifts off down her long hair and is lost

BUMPY KISSES: POEM

WRITTEN TO A POET (TO R—)

remember those bumpy kisses
in the back of that taxi
we should have begged the cabby
more hit more potholes please

when he hit a bad one whoops
everything got flung up hard
but don't some things just get better
by bouncing from lips to lips

kisses usually get their kicks
from boredom the normal routine
tongues stick in the same linebreaks
the proper punctuation in

but not these bumpy babies
they jack out the box they
jump all the jolts of this jaunt
lucky for us it's transient

after a poetry reading
briefly we'll share a ride heading
uptown toward distant lives
has one of us now arrived

still the course of our smoothest words
is likewise unpaved by poems
we scribble them down sometimes
hurried as hugs through a cab-door

through even they must go
past first dates or last we try
we mostly try and let them be
the moment they were meant to

RELICS WITH OLD BLUE

MEDICINE-TYPE BOTTLE: TO X

This old blue medicine-type bottle, unburied
From your garden last year's the perfect centerpiece
To suit our supper—the totem-trope we need
Across this kitchen table, to show how dangerous

It is where we sit (knees near touching at times)
Dawdling and playing with our silverware,
Tapping teacups, tired and satisfied and prime
From a stint in that garden: in a few hours

We'll find ourselves in bed, but we don't know that now,
Do we—we're still exchanging histories
(It's only my something visit to your house),
Just sorting out the portions of who, when, how—

Numbering the decades and the romances
That went bad, the faces that faded on us,
Though nothing too personal at first, just pain;
Divorces, liaisons, estrangements, fixations—

Of course our brows hurry away from hurt:
Anecdotes begun in wince end in wrinkly;
Our woeful tales go told through a mode that's mostly
A kind of moue, comic attitude, which flirts

With grimace-smiles, jokes, the mocking of those choices,
Those great mismatings: funny how it seems of late
Both of us have been alone, celibate . . .
Collating, getting our dates right, our voices

Shed their list of affairs, entanglements, crises:
So we accord the past its poisons, and theorize
That even this old blue bottle here, stored poisons
Before we were born: — followed by suggestions

That the toxin of those heartbreaks is gone
After this long, their vitriol has fizzed out,
And we could, given an occasion, again
Consume the spirit that killed us once, if not

The letter: confessions used as cue-cards to prompt
Mutual responses of empathy or hope:
No former hemlock can harm us now — we're immune
By now — don't you agree — because what happens

Ripens in retrospect; each sour memory
Blossoming like the flowers you sometimes spruce
This bottle's corroded throat with. We certainly
Are not eating much, are we, but we don't notice —

Can't we see how our fingers will likewise bloom
From off these knives and forks and force their field,
Interlocking like tugged-at roots . . . Untombed
Of its venom, this blue vial vigils our held

Glances. Sieved in its acid, its distilled mirror,
Would we (almost as soiled as it by time) appear
A beauty, a scarred heirloom any collector
Might stuff high on a shelf amid simulacra—

Somber still, it approbates that emptiness
We must be preparing to fill with each other—
It foretells the coiled taste, the bite unearthed
In the antiquity of a sudden, wild kiss

Whose disclosure will surprise us, as if
We have not been wholly inured by the years,
The stories we bare here across the rice, the life
Stories bittersweet, neutered, too well-rehearsed.

Will deadlier words then surface—their potency
Dis-elixired, drawn; decanted so often
That by our courteous age they've turned as grimy
And bunged with dust as this blue glass was when

Your shovel showed it that summer morning, and
My phrases here are (surely) just as corrupt—
What matter its sharpness, no metaphor can
Pare the ground from us as hard as we try to dig up,

To excavate feelings a bottomless need for
Soars as we toss the salad greens and pour
Dressing dripping down their fineleaved freshness
Starting to wilt already around the edges,

To rot back to that mulch they burst from. Such decay
Preserves some artifacts, if not us: they lie in
Graves contrived to obviate the skeleton
They survive beside, they strive to deny

The obvious, the crepitude fate-of-flesh bleak
Facts of our demise, obdurate bricabrac knickknacks
Laid by ancients in the coffin to propitiate
Ancestors, to aid, via these vain trinkets,

(Are we the "subjective correlatives" of these
Objects, this chthonic junk the tomb-robbers missed,
Tools and talismans, amulets, a corpse-cache
Gear for ghosts, props to assist the posthumous)

Some afterworld sojourn of the soul entering
Itself, self dying to carpe diem one more day.
Refocus *us* on this figure, this table-centering
Blue bottle. Whose future dye indigos our day.

Dulled, we ignore these darker, gnawing warnings—
Our own skull-and-crossbone labels long since skinned—
We poke at our plates, we pat our napkins.
What antidote waits, withering, within

Against that great granulate upheaval of
Fields whose depths have grown archeological—
Filled by fucked relics and by that above-all
Most subterranean of discoveries, love?

SALON POEM IN LEAFGRAVURE

Cemetery statuary
ought to be deciduous: wings
that fall from angels every
year, all the cherubs losing
their curls, the harps their strings—

Or imagine graveyards in autumn
minus those high carved-out figures:
and not just the sculptures,
but names, dates, epitaphs. Each tomb
turned into a bare limb—

Each stone branch of the "ceme-tree"
would stand once more a slab
the better to weather tragically
another Dec-Jan-Feb.
Come springtime gallery by gallery

etched letter-buds could open
that blankest bark
where new-limned numerals would mark
those old lives' span,
and spranked up there above them

let crosses blossom,
the tall crosses regain
their nailed arms. Now all the chisel
foliage should follow until the whole
museum from within is risen.

TO JOSÉ LEZAMA LIMA

The poem is a letter opener that slices
a to discover b in which c waits
and so on until z reiterates
my metaphor's acute dullness, its crisis

of belief: say this knife could core its way
past the final alphabet and penetrate
that rind that blinds us with its consummate
yield of polished inveighed truths which betray

nothing of the stuffing, the seeds that rot
innate tumors of meaning, enemy
rumors amassed across your desk each morning—

what if that surfeit of words was a warning
label only, just another skin to be
cut? And all this is unless the poem is not.

VITAL SIGNS

Suicides are the pulse of time.
Its BP and temp are not, however,
Births and weddings respectively.

I respect all three, though;
I even regulate myself accordingly—
Because hours, even instants,

Require our belief or else
They will become forever;
The transitory needs us to pledge

Ourselves to its exit, yet this is a typically
Poetic phhft-thought, a whish of words,
A Rilkemilky blancmange.

The ground breaks off a bit of dust
To give to us, a little crust
For the lips of the lost.

AN INSTRUCTOR'S DREAM

Many decades after graduation
the students sneak back onto
the school-grounds at night
and within the pane-lit windows
catch me their teacher at the desk
or blackboard cradling a chalk:
someone has erased their youth,
and as they crouch closer to see
more it grows darker and quieter
than they have known in their lives,
the lesson never learned surrounds
them; why have they come? Is
there any more to memorize now
at the end than there was then—
What is it they peer at through shades
of time to hear, X times X repeated,
my vain efforts to corner a room's
snickers? Do they mock me? Forever?
Out there my past has risen in
the eyes of all my former pupils but
I wonder if behind them others
younger and younger stretch away
to a day whose dawn will never
ring its end, its commencement bell.

STUMPED

I wish I could count
up to one without
first cutting off
nine of my fingers

THE SCULPTURE (TO —)

We stood there nude embracing while the sculptor
Poked and packed some sort of glop between us
Molding fast all the voids the gaps that lay
Where we'd tried most to hold each other close

Under the merge of your breasts and my chest
There remained a space above the place our
Bellies met but soon that clay or plaster
Of paris or state-of-the-art polymer

Filled every hollow which we long to fit
Then we were told to kiss hug hug harder
And then our heat would help to harden it

We stood there fused more ways than lovers know
Before the sculptor tore us away
Forced us to look at what had made us so whole.

PRISCILLA, OR THE MARVELS OF ENGINEERING (A FATAL FABLE)

A "Swingles Only" Cruise to souths tour on the
S.S. *Priscilla*: parties, spurtive romances, confided
Antiperspirants, quickchange partners. Suddenly
3rd day poolside blank, sun
Ouch I meet up a daze dish somehow haun't
Crossed my eyes' equator yet: she preened
To have appeared out of that presumptuous
Nowhere our hoarse soggy captain's
Nailed in place on his compass: in all the swarmy sticky
Nightlong pairings-off, secret lifeboat
Drill assignations, where did you come from
I offered haven't laid uh eyes you behind musta been blind. Oh
I've been around she said, I've seen you operating
That blonde last night, har, har, har.
Flattered, I introduced my name's Bill. Priscilla.
—As in S.S.? We laughed over the coincidence,
Wringing fragile martini chill stems all
Around us similar neo couples were
Gangplanking each other, coral lounge dusk deck.
Dinner, we promised. Then the moviedance,
Then . . . ? Our eyebrows guessed "The night?"
Separating to change, we hugged all sprinkly

But at table that PM I stained her napkin but

She didn't show up went looking for wasn't at the dance

Either. Hmmph, not on deck—where could she

Be? I asked all the other cats and chicks

Where the hell's Priscilla? describing her. No way

Man ain't never seen no piece like that since we

Ask the purser—man you sure? Tête-

Â-tète sure, I replied. The purser!

I'll get her cabin number, she might not be feeling

Oh boy I didn't inadvertently slip a torpedo into her drink that

Stud I scored from said they work every,

The purser. But no señor

There is no Priscilla everywhere listed amongs

The passenger list I'm jorry. The boat—she

Is S.S. *Priscilla*? he added helpfully, concerned, as though I were
    nutlong no

No you nit-tit—she has to be on look I met her this

Safternoon in the "Cock 'N' Tail" Lounge. Jorry

Is no let me have that thing here on the passenger look for jourselve.

Damn! she ain't on it

A stowaway hunh

That's even better

I'LL get her

She can't escape what's

Gonna do—hide in the ocean?

But

Finally, frustrato, angry not even drunk after no

Go searching all night, at sailor's dawn I slunk to my cabin and

Guess who I found the bitch all tucked up in that little cute-ass

Type beds they have Priscilla!
I hissed. Come to bunk
She swelled. But you, you aren't . . .
Aren't what, know whatcha're crazy dam—
Shh let's love she swayed. Okay: I'm game. 'Sbout time. So we
Start fucking but her movements were too calm
And rocking, elusive as chase in tune with the ship's
Wash on the waves. Gentle, coaxing, mocking-
Musky, chromosome-zoney, internal
As sea. It was eerie
The ex of it cited
Frightened me. My Y shot up: I began
Fug and fury ramming, I urged
Harsh thrash strokes, I hard
To hurt her with my penis, I remembered
That Norman Mailer story where he calls his "The
Avenger" I was pissed, make me
Frantic look all over the goddamn
Ship you cunt slammed all my spite ptooey
Into her. And then, and then . . . instantly . . .
Something . . . all I know is I came the split
I hit the water. I was drowned, of course,
In the famous shipwreck. The famous shipwreck
You remember
It was in all the TV—
Shots of it sunk in shallow clear just
Off an atoll. And everyone aboard was lost, adios,
Unusual or not unusual in these cases. But no one
Nobody could figure out how

The S.S. Whatshername had
Gotten all those great big gaping holes
Ripped, slashed, torn in her hull nor
What caused this deadfall rupture, the grievous eely capsizing.

Couldn't have been a iceberg
That
     far
        south.

SONNET (TO ——)

The way the world is not

Astonished at you

It doesn't blink a leaf

When we step from the house

Leads me to think

That beauty is natural, unremarkable

And not to be spoken of

Except in the course of things

The course of singing and worksharing

The course of squeezes and neighbors

The course of you tying back your raving hair to go out

And the course of course of me

Astonished at you

The way the world is not

WISHING WELL

I weigh the coin in my palm
against the water's clarity
that shines up at my shadow:
what wealth to smash apart that calm

gleaming, stake my greedy claim
on the future, my need to go
rewarded with all I owe.
I stand above the well to see

whether such a small as this
sacrifice is worth one wish—
the water is cold and stony
to a depth I can only guess.

And even if it reaches that far,
plummeting through the rich
rings of its sinking to reach
a bottomlessness whose core

is death's perhaps deepest ore,
there where the end gathers
will my silver ever bring me
any of the gold it shatters?

LIFER (AKA "HAPPY BIRTHDAY")

our prisoner
has received a package
containing a cake
which of course he thinks
must conceal a file
or a hacksaw-blade
and starts
to dig down into

actually however
his salvation
his way out
his escape route
has been carefully laid out
in brightcolored frosting
over darker frosting

the crucial message
the delicate pinkly lettering
overlooked
unheeded
falls shredded apart now
by his hopeful search

MIZU NO OTO

Pain passes for sunlight at some depths
which most of us never strike; the dive
is too far: or is the ear sheer enough—

Basho by a pond heard a frog make
the usual faucet-dripping-into-a-keyhole
sound; it wisely ignored his efforts

to collaborate. Get our galleyslaves
rowing with icicles for oars, that's
one way some say. Resist the urge

to halve the sea/be laser Moses,
to submerge yourself as a slice
speciman, all random camera words.

Beyond the caprice of earth to slake,
thirst issues from the source it breaks.

OVER AND OVER

A child recites the alphabet
but you in years still hard to get,
your rote is what I memorize.

It's you these counted words revise—
and say that today's forays, they
hazard voyage, do you care for sure?

Alone now with the old shapes that
bless tables bare, can't you wait,
wait for A to begin anymore—

how ache with alacrity you say
every tide is an advent, a day,
and too many days is the sea,

though the sea is day. Unique
with frequent stays you repeat.

ANCIENT MEASURES

As much as someone could plow in one day
They called an acre;
As much as a person could die in one instant
A lifetime—

MINOR POEM

The only response
to a child's grave is
to lie down before it and play dead.

CUES

The pain in my shoulder feels
like maybe 600 dpi; its needles
are printing out a text in a tongue
I can't read, a tongue with no tongue,
no flesh, only bone, my skeleton
signaling via these arthritic jottings
how soon it will replace this English
with its chill Cyrillic. An ur-language
honed to finitude, earth parlance
of a planet ultimately diminishing
into the dust of galaxies, utterance
from the Big Bang, which probably
made no bang, no sound, only
the auditory equivalent of a pinprick,
kin to these jabs stabbing poking
the nerves near my neck. Even
if I knew the comebacks to these cues,
would they alleviate any ache at all?

WINDOWBEAM

Ray that overruns every pane,
force that first invades but then

is pervaded: sunstripe penetrant!—
what made your phalanx fail: why can't

its gallant-greaved angels'-armor
avert our dirt: must the conqueror

convert his ways, the savior adopt
savage customs? We slaves corrupt

all bright kings—each mote of us
holds abject thought that blots with dust

your gold-shed greatness: shadow
breaks your arc and essence. How

transient the transparency
you brandished here so recently.

TO LIVE BY

Work from the original toward
the beautiful,
unless the latter comes first
in which case
reverse your efforts to find
a model worthy of such
inane desire.

Even the mouth's being
divided into two lips is
not enough to make words
equal themselves.

Eavesdroppers fear
the hermit's soliloquy.

Wake up, wound, the knife said.

MY LIFE BY ME

Every autobiography
longs to reach out
of its pages
and rip the pseudonym
off its cover.

WORSE

All my life I had nothing,
but worse than that,
I wouldn't share it.

DECASYLLABICS

Condign rightly I get shot down each time
I violate the No Poetry Zone,

always the NPZ (otherwise known
as the world) curtals me with hush command:

one foot and I am trespass in that land,
where the prose police have standby orders

to kill me should I dare breach its borders,
or if I even err to breathe in rhyme.

FEARS (CONT.)

niche niche niche niche
the birds go seeking a covert

eclipse eclipse eclipse eclipse
my shadow hides behind the sun

this this this this
every corner finds a crevice to keep

wish wish wish wish
the oldest word pacifies the youngest infant

Sometimes a dream will show me
the words I need to begin and end and
then take them away and leave just one
word or, like last night, three or four:
"the arms of care." That's all. There
were lots more but they vanished when
my eyes opened; they were of course
the words I need here now to justify
this. How can I forgive myself for
forgetting them, forgetting that which
might have made me whole for a while
holding you all in my arms of care?

PENNY WISE

well alright
I grant you
he was a fascist
ahem antisemitism the
er war and all
I'm not defending them
but at least
you've got to admit
at least he
made the quatrains run on time

INTRUSIONS

Sometimes I wake up to find
I have been scratching
the phone while asleep.

Sometimes I forget the letters
that make up my name,
that take down my word.

Afraid of such disowning, I eye
every passerby. Each is
a breach of my uniqueness.

(None of them completes me.)

Each of my pores is a different color,
but I am not any of those colors,
the pointillist told me. I stared

beholder at that older world.

EPOCHS

Even the tamest media trembles
When it hesitates to depict the gods
Raping and raging down on us mortals
Though as always the middle class applauds

Others fear this bestseller artistry
And they run hide between bare walls of earth
In such troubled times officials must see
An increase in myths of a virgin birth

If miraculously you can survive
Opening spring through its fine frozen doors
Hoping to catch any ally alive
Notice all the windows in the big stores

How they all show a swan bedded in blood
Her advertised blue eyes lidded with mud

NAOMI POEM (THE STARFISH ONE)

Each evening the sea casts starfish up on the beach, —
scattering, stranding them. They die at dawn, leaving
black hungers in the sun.

                     We slept there that summer, we
fucked in their radiant evolutions up to our body. Ringed
by starfish gasping for their element,

                               we joined to create
ours. All night they inhaled the sweat from our thrusting
limbs, and lived.

                    Often she cried out: Your hand! — It was
a starfish, caressing her with my low fire.

TWO OR THREE SITES

FROM A FAILED AFFAIR

Dozing while I dreamed on down your body
to where all fresh from a swim or a bath
I woke, seeing it still, that false witness,
that law they call displacement. Miles away
the reservoir was polluted by this—
I lay wondering in what water, who
can I be renamed renewed to lieu you.

In the desert, I insist that a soloist
waits hidden behind each dune which undulates
silent, lurking till far off the orchestra
starts, their wholescale music merged toward noon;

yet even here I have to swear I admire
that air of exaggerated effortlessness
conductors use to pick the baton up off its stand;
is this how to proceed when making love:

the over-implicit manner, the art concealed;
a strength of skills held in belial, reserved;
expertise on tap, an oasis of ease

somewhere deep: I've never been able to do it
I guess. Access I can't the virtuosity
to be both; both hesitant and satisfied.

Our bodies converged to bisect the bed,
dividing it lengthwise in half; too-brief
border, momentary truce contested
by the realms that spread on either side of
us; or a map, an antique tapestry,
split over sparring heirs. Death. Aftermath.
Whatever could have severed you from me?

MIRRORSHORE

If there were as many Melisandes for
each beach as fall through an hourglass
every eternity what time would the tide
in her tell me not to despair unless
I could no longer see their singular

Melodies or sands what would it matter
waking to hear their dirges praise
the years tatter demay the day when
echo believed its ears once too often
trickle trillions every second scatter

Love has too many skins for X to pare
skeletons prefer closeups in caricature
what a waste of shame's Shakespeare
if I cannot penetrate each hide of it
find some door core for my sill secret

New way I nail your soles to mine and
run out to find you though as always
I can't escape via a shadow that stays
straycaught in the fall from one to all
that's a sleeve-jest we'll share for a while

So tell me will the walls stand for ruin if
the ceilings those adolescents decamp
and finally what is it that separates
human from hum from hmm and um
from all my never-any Mels held quiet

Immersed in measure too template to trust
what dumb-long phrase thumb-print drains
if I take two steps for every step that flees me
will I end up here sad cellmate of sea
while the true she eludes these few grains

Always its mirror can shave me entire
the waves still have me dune by dune
if there were only as many here as her
should I care to character that the moon
in the water has the face of a deserter

BITTER THOUGHTS IN NOVEMBER

Every branch is more beautiful than
every other one, the rain falling or
the rain frozen pendant on this
twig I break off to swizzlestick that

puddle in which winter is opening
its cracks like sky, glazing minutely
drop by drop in closeup glissade
each face I bring to its brink, each beauty—

In theory the maze ascends, its core
is heaven according to mystics whose
stiles litter the way. Style is a pun
and therefore leads to perdition downward

doubters claim. Poets/critics: the veins
get pissed on by the capillaries.

TO THE READER

I hope you die while reading this book
And then when your folks come in

With flyswatters and grins
They see the title in your hand and

Jump back ten feet land
In the garbagecan nearer oh god to thee

And then I hope they plant you still
Ahold of it so when the rats get going

They can use the pages for napkins
But if you do survive

This it only proves you're some kind
Of vermin worm only one of them

Could pore through a deadun's dirt
And live

ON A DRAWING BY CHARLES TOMLINSON

By a swath of inks the eye
thinks it sees solitudes
which alter with the watercolor
way his brush washes its dye

in distance, though even this
finds a faraway fixed not
by the surveyor's plumb but
by the action of the thumb

delaying all the fingers meant
to draw out the paper,
splashed dry. The clean grain

catches what it should retain
if enough pressure pleasure
is applied to the stain to lie.

POEM

They say the universe is expanding,
not staying in one place.
I, though, have a small rental room
somewhere in it.

I don't understand this ratio
of the whole being free,
while the parts struggle to cough up
on the first of the month.

What do you grow in that vase?
Shards.

I don't understand.
And my worth is not enough
to figure out why. Who.

What suffers such distance just to endure?

FOR LACK OF YOU (TO —)

I examine the sun's diagrams
for your tan. The ground's plans for your walk.
Sky's project-papers on how, where
to utilize your breaths. All these schemata,
endless as my tracings of your faraway
face—poring over them in a solarium
observatory devoted to the study
of you. New proposals, outlines to
blueprint each movement: slowly reading, hoping,
finally I grow feeble-eyed. The fineprint for
your lashes, the arms' down, fades. Now
you're abstract, a block, an architect's
whitest nightmare or any bare construction of
skylines, vague unhouseholds. The plumbing
venues, vent of window or door
vanished, even the light itself a blur—
at last comes total blindness:
touch-awkward I feel like an ogre, a clumsy giant
tripping upon some ruins,
rubble of the town he's just smashed.
Tower-cursing as I bang my knee. Or no:
I'm tiny. I can see again! I see the giant walk off
favoring his one leg . . . favoring

my one you, I kick through
the strewn clutter; I get down on all fours
and start to scour around: one model, just one
to copy from, to begin again. That's
all I need, lacking you.

STREET

Down the street children run in circles—

A balloon laughs with a string in its mouth.

Why am I still interested in what lies at the bottom

Of my yawns of boredom?

No, I should not probe so.

Living on pavement pensions,

A mid-husband to the mis-wife of my breath.

In a doorway a savior pauses to straighten his stigmata.

Entering or leaving?

The choice leaves one speechless,

Groundless. The tall voice in my throat totters

Like a tower from which two or three bricks fall to the sidewalk,

Causing hoarse dust to rise.

The dust that rises immediately begins to avenge this insult to its species.

THE PATRIOTS

at the edge of the city in
the garbagedump where the
trucks never stop unloading
a crazy congregation stumbles
from trashmound to trashheap
they smash their fists down on
whatever's intact they tear
to bits the pitifew items
that have remained whole they
rip everything old woe clothes
papers cans bones to nothing
with their shining teeth
the enlightened the faithful
every twelve yards one of them
falls and is torn to shreds by
the others at the edge of
the city where there's a line
waiting to join

THE DAWNING

Now it takes only minutes
for light to travel from
the sun to the earth,

but an eternity to go
just six feet further, down
to where the dead are,

yet I could arrive there
immediately if I left
right away, my journey

blink-instantaneous,
world by world unscreening
itself: if I shed all trace

of surface—unsoiled each
skin which holds me here—
if my rays suddenly

were allowed to blaze forth
against their distance in
whole less time than this,

although I know they lack
the lightyear's intuition,
the nova's needle's-eye,

I pray they penetrate
always the dirt and find
a place haven to our kind.

SNUFFED

The candle's leaf
is what we call those drops
that cling solidified
up along its length
after it's been blown out —

We switch on the overheads. Outside,
branches bode, bode, bode.
What
do they predict?

Descent is all,
they're not specific, unlike
our phrase
for this froze ooze
(which beads the bole)
(and which is more like sap than leaf)
this effluvium, this sheaf
that trickled from a flame we lit once
days or years ago.

Time, our sentence, is specific.
Memory, its syntax, vague.
The melt is where they meet —
inksoil syllables dribbling down a page.

MY THEORY

The universe's mission is to expand,
all scientists now agree; yes, but why
should that be its quest, they question—

Based on my experience, my theory:
if one remains in the same place, one
must pay rent, life's made me understand.

Landlords and clergy may disagree
with me, but look, see every galaxy
sneak out the back, starcase in hand?

ANOTHER FALSE EXECUTION

The crime-rate in our land is so great that
I could commit Murder A confident that
Simultaneously someone unknown to me
Would nearby be committing Murder B—

My plan's to confess to Murder B which should
Cover up my real guilt for A because if
I was busy perpetrating B how could
I have done A. The identical times of

The crimes and my evidentiary shame
Convince the law of that. The subsequent
Trial verdict shall hoistpetard my scheme,
Girding me with the gloat I'm innocent

Of that of which I stand condemned: I die
Endowed in the knowledge my sentence
Is wrong, thereby maintaining to the end
That moral superiority, that perfect high

Which is the cause of most crimes if not mine.

HAVENOT

Out of a dozen I prefer the one
That's most like thirteen, the one
Autumn drops its cease-colored nets on.

Out of a once I prefer the one
That never was, that eludes its own,
Twins peering at each other through keyholes.

Out of a one I prefer the none
Who has my face, who evens the end
And odds the origin. The belated begun.

Out of a most I prefer the many
Who are not me, who remain free
Of that disciple number, that slave figure.

Twelve nonce, thirteen's the tense, which fourteen ends.
Despite my choice, I have no preference.

HOLLYWOOD NIGHTMARE

Soon to be a major mirage, my face—my face
never changes! To look each day in the mirror
is boring as going on location shoots
or signing autographs for my stable
of fans or being typecast in detective
roles. Sigh. Sometimes all I do is sit by my pool

and spazz out until my brain is a black pool
of emptiness, my eyes reruns: until my face
wears the neutral mask of aura a detective
affects. And when I am blank as a mirror,
as dull, when I sprawl as snoozeful as a stable
full of saviors, I dream: I dream someone shoots

me and he becomes a celebrity. He shoots
me and he gets the house, the swimming pool,
the Andy Warhols, the Rolls, the Porsche, the stable,
the . . . the lawn he gets! Christ, it's like divorce. My face!
He gets my face too? He's like a fucking mirror
of me . . . ! Jesus, you'd think some goddam detective

would know it's not me: when I'm a detective
on screen I know who is who. The badguy shoots
the goodguy sometimes but when they hold a mirror

over the goodguy's lips you see a pool
of mist appear and then his pal the co-star's face
looks all relieved. Cut to the hospital: "Stable?"

the doctor smirks, "Yes: his condition is stable.
Of course, with the brainectomy his detective
days are history, uh hunh. His face? His face —
hell, our plastic-surgeon loves a challenge: shoots
these Before and After photos? Great stuff! . . ." The pool
of reporters from the Daily Sun Rhymes Mirror

yawns at the grinning doctor while in the mirror
above my white white bed I maintain a stable
noble absence; my non-being is a pool
of pure mystery — a sheer puzzle any detective
would arrest the cursed creator of: I see shoots
of lilac and crocus come bursting from my face

each time the mirror closeups. But no detective
can solve this daily dream, whose stable-cam shoots
me here beside my pool, here, inside my face.

MISHAP MESSAGE

I bandage my wristwatch
to stop the bleeding
of time but time
is perforce the wound
out of which space empties
Einstein's bag of marbles

the greenie I shoot at its sister the moon
the purey I bury with a note saying no
the blue one weighs in my hand
as light as sky minus earth
earth of course is the last marble

I like to hear it roll
around my showerstall
before I fall into the drain
into that distillate of distance we call
ocean

whitecaps whitecaps
beneath each of which
a nurse bobs up and down

cold fingers hold my wrist
cold toes probe my throat
is that my pulse I ask
sisters is that my life

is that the onomatopoeia of the waves
words that jumble space with time
laughter tumbling down a telescope

words that turn to marble all I say
white as my years they bleed
they bleed away
white but white as only Einstein's hair is white
or a note slipped under drowning doors

OCT-NOV (MICHIGAN MEMORY #4)

The bacon of the ankles crackles, and the sky
Perks up birds this coldsnap morning—every
Breath sheds a breath-effect, brief-bloomed steam-sheaf . . .
Puddles huddle in frost. Past the barn the path

Shoots hill-pastures which rose to winter early
And sun-shucked clouds blast off from: migrants that fly
South—mouths that wet-nurse icicles—hatch forth
A form, a furious precision I sloughed

At birth, preferring life. And like the wind
Can reduce anything to description—
Running to finish my chores, beneath my scarf

I'll feel my chinbone seek my collarbone,
As if the flesh has ceded and the skeleton
Now must precipice itself against all warmth.

POEM

Even when the streets are empty,
even at night, the stopsign
tells the truth.

BE

Nothing will justify
your sadness
or something will:

you long to shrink
to that bare level
where either is believable;

where both equally console:
shrivel ground where
her absence will not matter;

will not embody this
or that starkest idol,
where her absence will

not matter or apply
nor fill the whole sky—
where it will not be

the world's equal.

THE RETURN

Behind me someone stalks
with shovel and covers
every footprint with
a spadeful, all my faultless

tracks effaced by small
mounds of dirt that mock
my slowing walk and show
the graves where to excavate

themselves, to get their holes
ready for that lag-leg day
I shall have to halt in the heart
the pace of my stride

and turn and try and take
the first steps back . . .

TAUTOLOGICAL

I am not happy at present.
I have never been happy.
Has anyone ever been happy—

The syllogism does not follow.
There are others like me
Who have never been happy,

But we are a minority.
Most people have been happy
At least once in their life:

Maybe I too could be happy
If the few who are like me
In never having been happy

Would all become happy
And leave me alone, unique.

CLICK

From the bottom of my well
I see the sun and moon just
once a day, which is nothing

when compared to you above
who see them both so often,
so open-shared, so totally:

and yet I believe that in that
instant when daily the sun
and monthly the moon fill

my circle rim up there, I am
illuminated in a way you can
never be, quenched entirely

and all sealed in light. See:
I'm whole now. No cracks in me.

BOSTON COMMON, AUTUMN 2000

The Statehouse dome
is painted gold
to reflect the greed
that gilds everything
in this Capitol:
superfluous these leaves
turning their richest color.

No one is fooled,
not even me, unless
it's by all the green-sickly
bronze statues in this park:
have they been seen by Doctors
from the Museum,
have they been authenticated lately?

These could be forgeries,
the real ones trucked off by night
to some billionaire's
penthouse of horrors:
eyrie I aspire to—my lair, my home!

The trees' lottery tickets descend
and fill my hands
with more than I can spend.

BEDDYBYE

Just hope that when you lie down your toes are a firing-squad.

SPHINX

I'm sorry about your photograph
What happened was in my wallet
And in my hurry to exchange addresses
With the fleeing cognoscenti
Across blown combed sands in
My favorite frantic sighs and
My lips those fresh red lispberries
Chilled by all the applause of sahara
In my haste and despairing shouts
Thrown back in my pocket my storm my lips
Musta dropped out
Musta been overtaken for lost for good
Like a dismembered shroud.

But slurprise
I got my wallet back in the windmail today
All there
The money and everything
The whole trillion billion
In gold dust and i.d. dew and
Gulp the only thing missing was
You of coursed it you.

Yum. Smack. I guess nobody
Nobody could be that honest.

LETTER TO A LANDSCAPE

How I painted you, first offering the blank
canvas a cigarette and a blindfold—
my execution left your image staring
into a space it could no longer mime
or defend with repeated acts of absence.

From now on destruction must be final.
The hole in the wall its nail made would cease
to suffice the clamor of the audience
stirred forward past their poses, a pittance
attendance. Let the cheaper seats applaud.

Massacre of semblance, matchless frame, perched
purloin to yield your past vast-hold, greenscene
that dangles there its last furtive hope of
grace-exit, set to vanish in the next
text which avider cliques click into view.

What scar has interhearted us with face
ruses the thousand roved letters I wrote
might have mentioned, those naive notes wrought-core
in similar airs to you, simpleton
valley, fall hive of greenery, high halt

desultory vista. Was it nine noahs
ago I boarded the wombship time, coupling
twain each mainseed of my father's crime,
garrotted-gored by his umbilical sword,
bride-groined bled. Now my yearyawns keep reading

kleenex for the word (sought as one, it dims;
wrought by many it screams) that would have freed
me until, terrified by such tearducts,
lamp-febrile, knees I lie in the wither
of wait. Near-antiquity these means.

Wholly articulated yet unsaid, reader-shaped
words appear before me, they come down the street
like all neat, if my lips could only tell you what
you hear them say, but let it settle gelid and
quiver-caught, the thought. Let it dupe a while.

Let it nought. Let it come nought. How loud
the brake that woke that word was. The sun sipped
us up through its thermometerstraw for
refreshment but summer days are so long,
so memoir. Like unsusbtitled foreign

films its landscape lacks meaning, each tree reflects
the alien dialog the actors exchange,
correspondent to your confusion, a child
told to not trust strangers. That's why I feel
the letter "I" would like to read itself as

everywhere epitome, but suspicion
is none to the person who inhabits
these crumbs, or so my cyber-bye eyes cry.
Each playdate of pellucidorean arbors
whispers past the hands berate I'll never grasp

alive the death around such carnal preen
artesian tensions. Its mirrors opaque
with old wisdoms of touch. See that sky seeping
hourglassly upon my closer eyelids
while my more distant ones blur. Infancy,

realm whose vacant aprons reared and shed name
welcome: a wonder of no thanks rowed the snake's
sidle sinuous canoed through the page of
far-eternity, bound fawning in toe
to you: tar vomit covers day with. Let snow

unsheathe those peaks earth holds above our craned
up beaks to learn how sharp such echo-other
heights keep their prospects honed, each precipice
razorboned must thrust all lapidary mist
that clings unstoried to that summit: my pane

re-sinews bleakly every breeze from up there.
Each brushstroke I heap you with is broken
by its cry. Aspirations try, but why, why
does Hiroshima always forget to duck?
Let landscape stand for letter. Let it lack.

WATER

you ask me why I come among you to mourn you

I say: I am the mourner

but we are not dead or dying

well: I am the mourner

we aren't afraid of you

I know: I am the mourner

but what do you mourn then if not us

not you: I am the mourner

is there anything worth mourning but us

yes: I am the mourner

when you leave us do you continue to mourn

to mourn: I am the mourner

your answers are only echoes

to echo is to mourn: I am the mourner

we won't feed you you know you'll starve

I live on lament: I am the mourner

but we are young and strong we don't need you

I am the mourner

here's a dollar beat it

thanks: goodbye

where will you go from here

there are others to mourn: I am the mourner

wait a sec is that all don't you have anything else

to say to us

I say: I am the mourner goodbye

wait you can't leave it like that

no: I have finished mourning you

hey wait up—stop—you fraud you—cheat stop

you catchgrief you thief

sorry: you have been mourned as much as you can be

but don't worry:

I am the mourner

POEM

when he woke in bed
it was 12 by the stones
that fell on his head

it was none by the night
and all done by the day
in either case it was too late

now a picture of his pores
handpainted on his bones
may show the way to others

shuttergrids of his face
promise pretty much that
yes he existed times space

his cup was both hands full
you can see it in the photo

Poland Through the Centuries a touring
Exhibition of maps drawn
By German and Russian cartographers reveals
There never was a Poland.

POEM

Night, in whose death did your ennui take refuge?

The women all lay their kerchiefs on the water, and stepped back.

THE RETRIEVAL

In order to recapture
the features of the one
lost, one must gaze
first into nothingness—

in which the semblance
encountered should
be blank, so it can flit
across the screen of

expectation, and wither
all the images there:
as we scan the past for
someone any the same

we could seem cipher
enough to erase each
old recognition held
so long in our mind.

The search necessitates
losing the present to
the degree we pursue
its opposite. The ratio

may not go exact, though,
and we may lose more
time than we regain,
the numbers may not

even out. There can be
an excess of loss, a gap
that greets us when we
return to our senses

clutching whomever
we've brought back to
a cache-void which can't
be filled by the thus

recalled person no
matter how beautiful
they hover here now
in place in face of us.

INSIDE OUTSIDE

I too will hang my coat in the closet
telling it to ignore the quizzical shoes
below, their wondering mouths agape.

When my ten fingers have finished
sharing me equally among themselves,
shall I at last grasp something whole—

Each of my scars has been tattooed on
an egg, then the eggs placed in tiaras
on hilltops. Horses surround the horizon,

solar pegs. Roan-ironic tree-scapes. Night
is when clocks enter and leave. But time
occupies me in exit. In exit only.

I hang here. Sky drips from the ceiling.
Why don't you understand my feelings.

POEM

There must be in the world still
Somewhere a lion could get me,
Or a cliff whose rocks might fall
(Struck by lightning) to crush me—

But wouldn't that be disloyal to
The carcinogens in my food air water
To whom I have promised my death,
The favor of killing me eventually—

It's nature versus culture: if we
Use the former to off ourselves with
(Running into tiger cages/snake galleries),

Won't the latter feel like a child
Abandoned (boohoo) by its parents?—
After all, we fathered these tinytot toxins.

FROM A DISTANCE

If lip-readers move their lips when
lip-reading, what do they say then?

Are the phrasings of the speaker
they scan claimed and mirrored there

unconsciously, an almost silence
less translation than transference?

Unless the mouth gets taken, sent
by its attendance to a strange intent

till even a cough, a kiss—enunciations
which paraphrase the space which runs

through all speech though all tongues try
to gun that gap by perusing, musing

mere coherence. Cued to its cusp,
these words of ours are less than lisp.

PLAZA DE LOCO

It's high tide in the hero
The floodgates fail the heart cowers
Blood of his deeds drowns the town square
Above it all this statue towers

And as the captain of a sinking ship
The instant the waves touch his toes
Snaps to attention it waits
Commanding some former pose

The inscription on which is blurred
Hey what is that word
What does his crumbling mad pedestal say

To find my way to you is
To not find your way to you
Therefore is not to find the way

ITINERARY

I pace off my heart,
six this way, six that way,
the length of a small wait
or a cave behind glass.

Quenching my teeth in shouts
I advance little by little,
late by late.

They open the door
emptier each time I pass,
they: the measured threshold,
the keyhole's spider groin.

Bury the dawn in ambush,
let white curtains count for home.
Make ruin my own.

NO WONDER

There is nowhere in the United States
Where you cannot arrange a murder
For a couple of thousand dollars or
Less, she said. This was Des Moines, Iowa,

But I can't remember the occasion—
I can't even remember her name, or what
Her eyes looked like when I kissed them
Or most anything else, except this.

Forgetting is a kind of murder, I guess.
But if, as my mom said about writing poetry,
You don't get no money for it why do it?

And why this poem; failed mnemonic
That costs me less than its insipid desire
To seem sincere, seem serious, does.

PEBBLES

I never try to do what those in the other arts do,
composers, painters, and them,
I only try to do what other poets do,
except when other poets try to do
what those in the other arts do,
in which case I don't.

BURIAL SCENE

On this shoveled open edge
On this lip of all our dreads

Earth seems most at balance
With its contending elements

The sun the cloud the wind the soil
All four exert an equal pull

So when the coffin enters
It presents no dissenters

Dressed in empty suitclothes
All mourners are scarecrows

Too far apart each one stands
Thus when they reach out hands

They can barely brush their
Limp glovetips against each other

STRESS THERAPY

Time, time, time, time, the clock
vaccinates us,
and then even that lacks
prophylaxis.

Ticktock-pockmarked, stricken
by such strokes, we
get sick of prescriptions
which work solely

on the body.
Systole diastole—
It is by its very

intermittency
that the heart knows
itself to be an I.

NONSENSE SONG

Mother-of-pearl, where is
your child-of-pearl, inside, and how,
who'll say, worn away perhaps
by so much worth?

Upshot white of hail's hold,
unhalved from issue whole,
world nacre-torte rolled
in sheets where no breakers foam—

Say what wave is ours,
what home. Now your shadow
is one of the shallows of light.

On whichever is the far side
of the eyelid I see it. I pray
my tongue may be your mouth's hermit.

POEM

Please, no dreams tonight.
No transfigured eyelids,
No siren rain
From the day's clouds.

Let the moon
Be boarded over.
No mirrors must signal
Their ally the wishwell.

Let there be nothing
For our faces to open in
But themselves.

Seen in this least light
They may appear
At last to be whole.

POEM

Doesn't each tree throw
its shade to show
boundary to the others'
thirsting thrust?
Only the roots are brothers;
the roots are the forest.

ON PAPER

in some ancient scriptures
every word in the text has
so many meanings that one
parable exhausts the thesaurus

candlesticks ablaze
on a wedding-dress's train
retreating over cobblebubble streets
light our way to the matter dome

paratroopers have slightly shifted
the dance diagrams on the floor
of the slaughterhouse next door
to capitalism's next move

just a few of the things I felt
worth mentioning to the page

PRESCRIPTIONS

I am watching, like the moon on a shelf,
How many days any I can still be myself,
And how few you. That being to whom
We browed our faces may recall such lackadaisia—

Circus horse scissors can snip yours across
A thousand screens, but can you skim from
Them the one you are or the nine hundred
Ninety-nine you remain to be? Fire engines

Pass with all our silences working furiously
Within, red as a guillotine blushes when
It contemplates the soul. Danton, Robespierre—
The way their lord swims among them in

Turtle purples of fear makes whole Paris bright.
Nightly the Terror bakes me, stale loaf of
Laughter: and already in my bank/my bastille
The time-locks all have long white beards—

Drawing maps across zebras may cut
The cartographer's workload in half, but
Me, I screech to a halt before a hypnotist's socks.
I am watching like the moon on a shelf

How many pablums remain in my RX,
And how many more pillowfights in marshes
And marshmallow fights in pillboxes
Have I to endure? La Revolution forever!

Otherwise I was abandoned long ago,
When I drank the flying ore of an hourglass. So
Please don't lie beside me asking the stars
Have you no other names to take but ours.

I paint everything over on its mouth.
Behold the hill from which all heights are felled.
Before throwing them I always gargle the dice.
Meanwhile they pile up, the medical bills.

ANOTHER HAIRBRUSH POEM

the hairbrush can hardly breathe
it suffocates in strands
it snarls as tense as teeth
biting an enemy's hands

the things we tame are what
entangle and turn us wild
every parent grows ragged tugged
disciplining their child

pity the year-old hairbrush
its stems all split its roots bare
like a field that's tilled too much
now a hoarbrush blooms there

hairbrush hairbrush have you
any tufts to spare today
now that I'm bald and cannot comb
please give back my gray

the hairbrush yanks and yanks
stubborn curl it won't lie dead
even a poorbrush has to shed
all the rebels from its ranks

(so try not to cry and just say thanks
when it hauls you off your head!)

QUESTIONS

Before we're born we're
lowercase, and after we die,
we return to it. Only life
renders us in capital letters.

(Every headstone ms.
should really be edited
by clones of e. e. cummings.)

Life is caps for the usual reason,
an exaggerated sense
of the significance
of one's thoughts.
Life is a Beat poet.

Upper existence or
lower nonexistence,
I'm sure the eye adjusts its focus
toward either case—

But which is easier to read—
greatness or goneness,
headline or poem?

Life or its foreward-afterward?

AGING INTO THE AVANTGARDE

When the mirror paints itself,
how true to life
the results seem—
But when it paints others, well,
take me, I who have posed so long
my patience has earned
the most flattering
exactitude: so why
(as the years go by)
is there this blurring
appearing where my face is;
is expressionism occurring?

When it comes to its own
likeness, it's photorealism no less—
the mirror paints itself
perfectly, whereas
the one it does of me
(I can see now as I lean closer)
in the end turns out to be
nothing but a sort of art brut:
the brushstrokes grow
more fauve, more cobra
each time I look.

THERE'S THE RUB

Envying young poets the rage
You wish you could reverse your night
And blaze out born on every page
As old as them, as debut-bright.

Child of that prodigal spotlight
whose wattage now is theirs to wage—
What gold star rite you wish you might
Raise revised to its first prize stage.

But listen to my wizened sage:
He claims there's one disadvantage
Should time renew you neophyte—

There'd be one catch you'd hate, one spite:
Remember if you were their age
You'd have to write the way they write.

MERRY-NO-ROUND

The wooden horses
are tired of their courses

and plead from head to hoof
to be fed to a stove—

In leaping lunging flames
they'd rise again, flared manes

snapping like chains behind them.
The smoke would not blind them

As do these children's hands:
Beyond our cruel commands

The fire will free them then
as once the artisan when

out of the tree they
were nagged to this neigh.

THE CONSOLATIONS OF

SOCIOBIOLOGY (TO —)

Those scars rooted me. Stigmata stalagmite
I sat at a drive-in and watched the stars
Through a narrow straw while the Coke in my lap went
Waterier and waterier. For days on end or

Nights no end I crawled on all fours or in
My case no fours to worship you: Amoeba Behemoth!
—Then you explained your DNA calls for
Meaner genes than mine and since you are merely

So to speak its external expression etcet
Ergo among your lovers I'll never be . . .
Ah that movie was so far away the stars melting

Made my thighs icy. I see: it's not you
Who is not requiting me, it's something in you
Over which you have no say says no to me.

POEM

Age retracts me, filling my hands
with shirtcuffs as I shrink, reduced
to secondchild. My skin is
smoke from a paper house, my hair.

Prepare a needle sea for me to walk on.

(Prepare me. Make sure
my cries are wrapped up in a leaf.)

(SERGEY) (YESENIN) SPEAKING

(ISADORA) (DUNCAN)

I love Russia; and Isadora and her dance.
When I put my arms around her, she's like
Wheat that sways in the very midst of bloody battle,
—Un-hearkened-to, but piling up peace for the earth
(Though my self-war juggles no nimbus). Earthquake; shoulders
A-lit with birthdays of doves; piety of the unwashable
Creases in my mother's gaze and hands. Isadora "becalmed"
Isadora the ray sky one tastes on the skin of justborn babies
(Remember, Isadora
When you took me to America
I went, as one visits a grave, to
The place where Bill Knott would be born 20 years in the future
I embraced the pastures, the abandoned quarry, where he would play
With children of your aura and my sapling eye
Where bees brought honey to dying flowers I sprinkled
Childhood upon the horizons, the cows
Who licked my heart like a block of salt) Isadora I write this poem
On my shroud, when my home-village walks out to harvest.
Bread weeps as you break it gently into years.

POEM HOLDING ON TO

A space whose whiteness has to be in quotes.

How we parted our names and pasted them
to a pebble too light for a paperweight
but now it circles the sun as I wake,
my worthless sought brought back to earth ways.

The time, day; the place, debris.
Beyond my description is nothing
but it means to do me harm.

All my steps few-transit the forsaken dew;
darkgutter caress, the leash of looks backward at me and you.

Fierce ice fenestrates the gap, cuts
a pane's penance across my faculty
forehead. Scalped scarecrow,
I wear an infant patina of voyeurs.

NAOMI POEM

The beach holds and sifts us through her dreaming fingers
Summer fragrances green between your legs
At night, naked auras cool the waves
Vanished
O Naomi
I kiss every body of you, every face

"QUOTE UNQUOTE"

Who wrote that we use our children to forget
the size of our parents, or is that really
a quote? And if it isn't, and if I forget
to write it, does that mean that someone will—

But what if someone forgets to write the words
that bring me here, that let me be born?
Oh micro-mini-soul, you, my shirking ego,
your quotemarks would just hang there in the air

like wings without a bird.

THE I DID

One memory from childhood
how when it was summer and hot
at ground level where I stood
above me I saw the tops of trees
palpitating in a proper breeze

that never came down to ease me.
I can't say I swan why I remember
what it is that makes it linger or
else enriches such a significant
nor could I see it now if I went

on a breathless day and looked up
I would not be far enough away
physically for the contrast: memory
needs that distance for its truth
to swerve from the present's path.

Is it right to hold the past fixed in
former attitudes like tops of trees
or whatever it is records history's
external focus switched to days
depictions drawn by winds upon

clouds or branches flexing wide
their leisure of purpose pause
from the hell of here. Sight cannot
even in summer when it is hot
share the air enjoyed by the eyed.

ALTERNATE FATES

What if right in
the middle of a battle
across the battlefield the wind
blew thousands of
lottery tickets, what then?

THE AVOWAL (HENDECASYLLABICS)

One's instantaneous grasp of the world must
Seem rare though normal as a day at the beach
With ocean's blank espousal bared beyond us,
Sounder than any words of semaphore reach

Even those few brave enough to share sudden
Care for adjacent strangers drowning aware
Their embodiment there's the same, some laden
Statistic of grief and amours, just one more

Devastating sentience. Echo canyons
Might flashback up every voice their steep rock flood
Flush with amnesia-enriched names, broke against—
Though I doubt we would be that whole if we could.

Are we near to express this and is that why
I'm feeling my way down a corridor of winks,
Nervous from all the lashes that brush me as I
Suffer due the narrow scrutiny of these ranks

Like cobwebs immense, humans really I guess—
Funny how most of us remain unfinished.
Me too, beautiful as all those who before
Being born vouchsafed their life to another.

HEGEMONY (PROSEPOEM)

In school kids would stand in back of me and stick two fingers up be-
hind my head to make the class laugh. Or so I was told. I took their word
for what had occurred and that it was universal. Due to its process, I
could not witness what had really happened or what it meant, what
made it funny. And I still don't know, even today: but I can feel them
back there, forefinger, middlefinger, ready to poke their putdown up for
the world to jeer me. That V looms always, that rabbit-ears or peace-
sign or whatever scourge-stigmata I pledge to represent; but what
hurts most is, I know that victorious viciousness only by inference,
only by report: I can never spin fast enough to catch a glimpse of it. I've
never been able not once to see this joke my entire life has suffered
the hands of. That's the worst part of this endless humiliation: that I
have to take it on trust, that I have to believe in it blindly.

THE WOULD-BE NONCHALANT

(PROSEPOEM)

I try to shrug it off, but when my shoulders poke themselves up to form the shrug they get stuck, and I slump down trapped inbetween these shoulder-peaks; so I live in the valley of a shrug, in its perpetual shadow.

AFTER THE BURIAL (PROSEPOEM)

After the burial I alone stood by till 2 workmen came to shovel the dirt back into the hole. There was some left over, the dirt she'd displaced, and they wheelbarrowed it off. Drawn, not knowing why, I followed at a distance. Coming to a secluded backlot, they dumped it, then left. I walked over. It made a small mound. And all around her, similar mounds. Pure cones of joy! First gifts from the dead! I fell to my knees before it, and fell forward on my hands into it . . . to the elbows, like washwater. . . . For the first time, I became empty enough to cry for her.

THE ALONE TONIGHT

I don't want to live with the alone tonight
Stay lost at home on my own tonight
But if I leave and go down to the street
The roads all throw their crosses at my feet
And words out loud the crowds all yell me
I don't want to die I hear them all tell me
And when their throats fall quotably quiet
Can I stand out dope and hope my own don't deny it
All songs are the same they show my shame in kind
The words are plain the pain finds its name in mine
It's no mistake I lie awake so straight and still
The maze I cannot penetrate waits at my doorsill
I could build bridges that make the sea blink
But there's no bank to build them from here on this nearside I think
They told me sold me how to live I had to buy it
But then they made me give up my seat in the riot
I don't want to live with the alone tonight
I'd love to reign on this throne tonight
I'm the empire at home on my own tonight
Habitat zone in my headphones tonight
The poems I wrote are afraid to quote me
Out loud that shroud of yowls won't save me
I don't want to live I hear them say daily
I don't want to die so please won't you say me
I don't want to stay please won't you play me

POEM IN THE CARDIAC UNIT

Time-charted, nursed, I let the meds
dictate this verse: roomriver rounds
take my pulse down stairwaves of stairs
scan my aches in chairbanks of chairs
and wake me on the bedbed of beds.

Multiplicities, pre-scripted;
metaphors bled, already dead:
what wouldn't be a cliché here—
paranoid mirror, bathroom sink,
flowing over with normal fear

as I squint at what I might mean
if I poeticized this scene: age
LSDs my chin; my once-lean
profile spills profilefiles, page
upon page rippling to see

even their prolific output
data can never sate the spate
pathoscopes that hardrecord spot
surveillance of what vital signs
remain in these veins, clotted lines

whose parse usurps my sleep. (Forget
how literate you hate this surge,
absurd, heartbeat creation; your
necknoun must stet its tide-edit
now, to quiververbs, wattlewords.)

What would my peergroup say, could they
modify this hyperguad gush,
advise my florid brainflushed flesh
stop pouring forth such images,
euphony beyond me. Sweet excess.

Is that not the gist this critic
monitor that beeps down its sic
keeps vying to brightly display
while I lie here less than what, what,
watched all night, till more's the day.

NOTES (BY BILL KNOTT)

ACKNOWLEDGMENTS

INDEX OF TITLES AND FIRST LINES

NOTES (BY BILL KNOTT)

29 ALFONSINA STORNI: Storni (1892–1938), Argentinean poet. In 1935 she was afflicted with breast cancer. A partial mastectomy did not keep the malignancy from returning, and Storni drowned herself in the Atlantic after writing a final poem, "Voy a dormir." The quote in lines 1–2 comes from a post-op letter: "I fear the cancer is on its way upstairs."

62 PEACE (PASCAL): "Most of our problems proceed from our inability to sit quietly in a small room." —Pascal

74 WIDOW/WIDOWER'S WINTER: Line 14 comes from a phrase I remember adults saying to me as a child when I dropped a piece of food on the floor: "Pick it up and brush it off—don't worry, you eat a peck of dirt in your life anyway."

85 ANOTHER FIRST KISS: TO X: Line 13: "Our age"—the lovers are fifty-three and sixty-one.

95 TO JOSÉ LEZAMA LIMA: Lines 10–11, "enemy rumors": Lezama Lima's second book of poems was entitled *Enemigo rumor*.

107 MIZU NO OTO: A meditation upon Basho's most famous haiku, whose final syllables I've used for the title.

119 PENNY WISE: Two puns explain the title and last line: "Penny wise, Pound foolish" And: Mussolini's admirers used to say, "Well, he may be a fascist, but at least he makes the trains run on time."

121 EPOCHS: After "Epoques" by Jean Follain. I worked from both the original and Serge Gavronsky's translation.

ACKNOWLEDGMENTS

Many people helped this book into print: Knott's literary executor, Professor Robert Fanning of the University of Central Michigan; Bill's assistant and friend in his last years, Leigh Jajuga; Star Black; William Corbett; Stephen Dobyns; Jonathan Galassi; and his friends and students at Emerson College—particularly James Randall, John Skoyles, Daniel Tobin, Peter Shippy, Jonathan Aaron, and DeWitt Henry. Shawn Delgado did some important and sharp-eyed transcription work early on in this process. Special thanks to my wife, Jennifer Holley Lux.

INDEX OF TITLES AND FIRST LINES

Poem titles are in *italics*.